Poets Thinking

Poets Thinking

POPE

WHITMAN

DICKINSON

YEATS

Helen Vendler

HARVARD UNIVERSITY PRESS
Cambridge, Massachusetts
London, England

Poems by Emily Dickinson are reprinted by permission of the publish-
ers and the Trustees of Amherst College from *The Poems of Emily Dick-
inson: Variorum Edition*, ed. Ralph W. Franklin (Cambridge, Mass.: The
Belknap Press of Harvard University Press, 1998). Copyright © 1998
by the President and Fellows of Harvard College. Copyright © 1951,
1955, 1979 by the President and Fellows of Harvard College. Poems by
W. B. Yeats are reprinted by permission of A. P. Watt Ltd. on behalf of
Michael B. Yeats.

First Harvard University Press paperback edition, 2006

Library of Congress Cataloging-in-Publication Data
Vendler, Helen Hennessy.
Poets thinking : Pope, Whitman, Dickinson, Yeats / Helen Vendler.
p. cm.
Includes bibliographical references (p.) and index.
ISBN 0-674-01567-3 (cloth: alk. paper)
ISBN 0-674-02110-X (pbk.)
1. English poetry—History and criticism.
2. Yeats, W. B. (William Butler), 1865–1939—Criticism and interpretation.
3. Dickinson, Emily, 1830–1886—Criticism and interpretation.
4. Pope, Alexander, 1688–1744—Criticism and interpretation.
5. Whitman, Walt, 1819–1892—Criticism and interpretation.
6. American poetry—19th century—History and criticism.
7. English-speaking countries—Intellectual life.
8. Thought and thinking.   I. Title.

PR502.V465 2004
821.009—dc22   2004047338

To the memory of
Elsie Duncan-Jones
devoted scholar, editor, teacher, friend

Church-bels beyond the starres heard, the souls bloud,
The land of spices; something understood.

George Herbert

Acknowledgments

THE ESSAYS IN THIS BOOK were originally delivered as the Clark Lectures at Cambridge University. I am grateful to Amartya Sen, then Master of Trinity College, for his sponsoring of my visit. He and Emma Rothschild made my time in Cambridge a happy and interesting one. Thanks are also due to Adrian Poole of Trinity College and the Faculty of English for his company and conversation. Old friends at Cambridge—the late Arthur Sale and Penny Sale, Eamon Duffy and Jenny Duffy, Heather Glen, Gillian and John Beer, Richard Luckett, the late John Stevens and Charlotte Stevens, and Chris Cannon, among others—offered welcome hospitality.

This book is dedicated to the memory of the Marvell scholar Elsie Duncan-Jones, to whom I last spoke on the occasion of the Clark Lectures. I first made her acquaintance on the page in 1948, when, as a young girl, I read the pioneering and brilliant book she had published (under the name Elsie Phare) on Gerard Manley Hopkins. Much later, in 1980, I was introduced to her in Cambridge, and we became friends. Her deep learning, her intense delight in poetry, and her infallible literary intelligence were radiantly communicated to all who knew her, and I count it a high privilege to have come into the precinct of her luminous generosity of spirit. We were brought together through the kindness of Dorothea Richards, whose husband, I. A. Richards, had first showed me how much a poem could express.

I studied Pope at Harvard University with the late Reuben

Brower, whose Augustan taste modified my notions of what poetry might be. The work of Wynn Thomas, of the University of Wales, has permanently influenced my sense of the delicacy and depth of Whitman's writing. The two profound teachers who introduced me to the work of W. B. Yeats, Morton Berman of Boston University and the late John V. Kelleher of Harvard University, are in my mind whenever, as here, I write about Yeats.

I wish to thank the outside readers for Harvard University Press for their helpful reactions to my manuscript. My expert editor, Margaretta Fulton, and my copy-editor, Mary Ellen Geer, have, as always, made the process of book-making a pleasure, as has the designer of this book, Marianne Perlak.

I am grateful to Yaddo for a residency in which I began to write the lectures that became this volume. There is no better spot in which to think and write, and no better company to be had while doing so. Michael Sundell, then the Director, and his wife Nina stood willing to facilitate their guests' work in every way, and the Yaddo staff made daily life easy.

My colleagues at Harvard offered valuable responses to the chapter on Emily Dickinson when I delivered it at a faculty seminar. I am grateful to the Department of English, the Dean of the Faculty of Arts and Sciences, and the Porter Professorship for funds for research, secretarial assistance, and computer supplies. The Harvard Library and the Library of Skidmore College are to be thanked as well, as is Herbert Leibowitz, editor of *Parnassus,* in which the Emily Dickinson essay appeared in abbreviated form.

My resourceful former assistant at Harvard, Lorraine Dardis, was a cheerful and sustaining presence during the time I was beginning this book. My present assistant, Alicia Peralta, has been a comparably deft and intelligent aide as I brought the book to completion. They are acknowledged here for kindness and helpfulness beyond the call of duty. And, as always, I thank the family and friends who, by making life worth living, make thinking and writing possible.

Contents

Poets Thinking

Introduction

Ashes denote that Fire was –
Revere the Grayest Pile
For the Departed Creature's sake
That hovered there awhile –

Fire exists the first in light
And then consolidates
Only the Chemist can disclose
Into what Carbonates –

Emily Dickinson[1]

THE PROCESS OF THINKING has usually been defined as a chain of argument, explanation, logical induction, or deduction. Thinking is believed to occur by way of proposed hypotheses, suggested evidence, and rational conclusions. Other mental processes—those of meditation, intuition, belief—are usually not granted the honorific name of thinking. Yet it is evident that many complex, and sometimes profound, operations of the mind must precede our final arranging of an argument, finding a path of explanation, or staging a deduction. We have names for some of these independent operations: classification, reconciling, sequencing. They are considered the underpinnings of thought rather than thinking itself, which is conceived of as an intentional set of rational linkages leading to a convincing result.

Poetry has often been considered an irrational genre, more expressive than logical, more given to meditation than to coherent or defensible argument. The "proofs" it presents are, it is judged, more fanciful than true, and the experiences it affords are emotional and idiosyncratic rather than dispassionate and universal. The additional fact that poetry is directed by an aesthetic imperative, rather than by a forensic or expository one, casts suspicion on the "thinking" represented within and by poetry. Since poems often change their minds as they proceed, they seem unreliable as processes or products of thought (Whitman: "Do I contradict myself? Very well, I contradict myself; I am vast; I contain multitudes"). By contrast to the more "permanent" assertions of philosophy or science, poets seem nonchalant about the durability of their affirmations (Yeats: "Things thought too long can be no longer thought"). The poets themselves have sometimes disparaged "consequitive reasoning" (Keats). And the waywardness of the lives of the poets seems to give the lie to their credibility as purveyors of wisdom. For these and perhaps other reasons, the word "thinking" is not often found in close relation with the word "poetry."

It is not obvious where "thinking" as such (by contrast to "inspiration") occurs in poetry. Is it part of "inspiration?" (But that word means "breathing in," a process hardly comparable to thinking.) Is thinking evident in the finished poem? A poem, after all, need not make an obvious argument; it need not adduce evidence; it need not assert a visibly new insight; it may be independent of a received cultural "system" (Blake: "I must create my own system or be enslaved by another man's"). A poem can be more lighthearted than the usual "thinking" process; it can be satiric, or frivolous, or mischievous. High seriousness may attend it—or may not. Bizarre imaginative fantasies may be what a poem has to offer; or "nonsense"; or some reduction of language that would normally be considered inadequate to "adult" thinking (Blake: "Little lamb, who made thee? / Dost thou know who made thee?"). Unlike the structure of a perspicuous argument, the structure of a poem may be anything but transparent, at least at first glance.

In short, the relation of poetry to thought is an uneasy one.

Some law other than the conduct of an argument is always govern-
ing a poem, even when the poem purports to be relating the un-
folding of thought. On the other hand, even when a poem seems
to be a spontaneous outburst of feeling, it is being directed, as a
feat of ordered language, by something one can only call thought.
Yet in most accounts of the internal substance of poetry, critics
continue to emphasize the imaginative or irrational or psychologi-
cal or "expressive" base of poetry; it is thought to be an art of
which there can be no science.

There have been in the past exceptions to this generalization.
I. A. Richards (principally in his teaching) exemplified a philosophi-
cally and philologically informed "close reading" of individual po-
ems (without, however, referring the phenomena he described to
characteristic authorial patterns); Northrop Frye helped to eluci-
date the order of thought manifested in literature, especially in the
narrative and dramatic genres, but he did not often pursue the
process of thinking within a single lyric; Randall Jarrell stressed
the feeling and expressivity of individual word-choice; William
Empson (although his focus on ambiguity rather militated against
a defense of poetic clarity) found the thinking mind intent on cre-
ating multiple levels of expression in complex words rather than on
evolving a line of inference or argument. One could cite others
among the New Critics who wrote cogently on lyric poetry, but
whose interest was not centered on the poet's ongoing thinking
within a poem: W. K. Wimsatt spoke for the force of rhetoric and
for the cognitive echoes (congruent and opposing) between words
that rhyme; Allen Tate and John Crowe Ransom argued for the
psychological complexity that produces "tension" and "paradox" in
both the substance and the texture of poetry; Cleanth Brooks and
Robert Penn Warren emphasized unity of structure and image and
the autonomy of the work of art. When a critic such as Kenneth
Burke focused on a single poem, it was to demonstrate a theoreti-
cal point (such as "symbolic action") rather than to remain with
the poem as an object, unique in itself, but participating in iden-

tifiable (and characteristic) authorial aesthetic patterns. More recently, we have seen the urgently voiced theory of Harold Bloom, whose practical criticism employs a discourse relying more on exalted assertion than on assembled evidence.

I learned, of course, from these admired critics (and was taught in my youth by Richards and Frye). I see in retrospect that my predecessors normally viewed a poem as an essentially static object, an entity that could be seen as a "verbal icon" (a stylized picture to be gazed upon) or as "a well-wrought urn" (an object with weight, solidity, and finite boundaries), or (in the case of R. P. Blackmur) as a "gesture" formed out of language, arrested in its signification. Although subsidiary notions of the poem as a "stream of consciousness" can be found in some of these critics (Burke and Bloom especially), in no case was the poem depicted primarily as a fluid construction that could change its mind as it proceeded. Nor was the poem seen principally as a work bent on following the lead of a law of aesthetic thinking, a work mimicking, in its motions, distinctive mental operations characteristic of its author. (The most comprehensive theorist of the fluid view of lyric has been the contemporary poet A. R. Ammons, not only in his poetry but also in his enlightening essays.)

I was, and am, more interested in developmental questions pertaining to an author's poetic oeuvre as a whole, and in single poems as examples of aesthetically directed fluidity, than I am in pursuing an all-purpose theory of lyric or a single aspect (rhetorical, imagistic) of technique. When, as a young student, I read literary critics, I longed for them to dwell on, and above all to explain, the aesthetic intent governing the unfolding of an individual poem, and wanted as well to see them track the aesthetic determinants of an entire oeuvre. What I did not find, I have tried to create—a criticism guided by the poem as an exemplification of its own inner momentum rather than as an illustration of a social, philosophical, psychological, rhetorical, or theoretical thesis. Criticism, I believe, while being alert to the smallest nuances of language-use, ought to infer from the text the emotional motivation that not only compelled a poet from silence into speech but also produced the originally unforeseeable contours of the evolving inner form of the work of art.

All poems, it seems to me, contain within themselves implicit instructions concerning how they should be read. These encoded instructions—housed in the sum of all the forms in which a poem is cast, from the smallest phonetic group to the largest philosophical set—ought to be introduced as evidence for any offered interpretation. In recent years, such intentionality has often been disregarded or resisted. The New Historicists, for instance, focus on contexts which, though perhaps relevant to the ideological contents of a poem, are irrelevant to its intrinsic processes. A "hermeneutic of suspicion" asks what social phenomena the poem may be concealing rather than by what aesthetic laws it may be constituted. The poem is too often conscripted into illustrating a social idea not germane to its own inner workings. And though any author is of course a child of an era, it is probably impossible to illustrate (with any credibility) an era by a lyric, or a lyric by an era: the grid is too small in the first case, too large in the second. It could be argued that the case changes when one considers the whole life-work of a poet—and yet what a poor use of Whitman's inventive genius it is to look to his poetry for large inferences about civil war or American democracy or nineteenth-century materialism. All that is remarkable in him tends to vanish when he is used as a means of cultural illustration, and his poems of less ideological relevance, under this treatment, sink without a trace.

For a relatively brief period, deconstruction—correcting the overemphasis on the poem as a system of integrated tensions or a static icon or a linguistic gesture—brought, in the work of Paul de Man and subsequently Barbara Johnson—a welcome attention to the temporal raveling and unraveling of thought within poetic texts (while usually preferring texts more extended than lyric ones). On the whole, critical theory—so dependent on anterior philo

sophical, social, or economic ideas for its own infrastructure—
has been uninterested in lyric. Theory operates better on the wider
sweep of narrative, philosophical writing, autobiography, and
drama; it has not found useful (for its purposes) the privacy of lyric
space, the symbolically condensed and abstracted function of lyric
language, and the resistance to social or philosophical systems in
the development of a poetic oeuvre. "Intellectuals" and their
"ideas" (invariably expressed in prose) occupy at this moment a
privilege in academic and popular discussion which is (absurdly)
denied to poets and poems—as though poetry and responsible
ideation could not, or did not, overlap.[2] "Great books" curricula,
while including epic and narrative poetry, have on the whole sup-
pressed the very presence of lyric in Western literature, as though
lyric poems had nothing to contribute to thinking.

To counter the common practice of separating the idea of lyric
from the idea of responsible thinking, I want to illuminate, if possi-
ble, the way thinking goes on in the poet's mind during the process
of creation, and how the evolution of that thinking can be deduced
from the surface of the poem—that printed arrangement of lan-
guage that John Ashbery has brilliantly called a poem's "visible
core."[3] I also want to demonstrate how a poet meditating on a
given topic often thinks serially through the topic by reframing it
in poem after poem, creating an active process of thinking that
generates as a result the entirely different structural inner shapes
those poems adopt.

Within poems, a drama is formally enacted by which we can ob-
serve a mind generating forms in an excited state; we participate in
that drama as we are worked on by the linguistic processes in view.
As is often said, but as often forgotten, poems are not their para-
phrases, because the paraphrase does not represent the thinking
process as it strives toward ultimate precision, but rather reduces
the poem to summarized "thoughts" or "statements" or "mean-
ings." Because the highest poetic achievement is the gaining of
an unmistakable, idiosyncratic, and formally coherent personal

style—extending to all planes of the poem from the imaginative to the musical—it follows that on the plane of thought poets will not resemble each other, that they will devise characteristic and recognizable patterns of thinking, which may themselves change over time, of course, but will also exhibit within each poet a psychological continuity. Because each poet is so distinctive in patterns of mental expression, my topic—poets thinking—cannot be generalized, but must be approached poet by poet. My case histories here are four.

In the case of Alexander Pope, I show a poet thinking (as he composes the *Essay on Man*) about a certain genre (the philosophical essay) and its characteristic form of discourse (assertion followed by exemplum). Pope asks himself how to create a poetically interesting version of the exposition of received "philosophical" ideas, with the aim of revealing (as philosophical essays decidedly do not) what thinking is "really" like as it happens. By miniaturizing and parodying intellectual discourse, he makes visible the sort of thinking that vividly occurs within his own mercurial and satiric mind.

In the case of Whitman, I focus on the genre of reprise (a frequent one in his poetry), in which something is articulated once, and then articulated again. This genre is provoked by a rethinking that motivates and enacts a second, aestheticized and more intellectual presentation of an earlier-sketched perceptual scene. I consider in passing both the advantages and the dangers of the reprise form: its advantage in representing the supervening of the aesthetic on the impressionistic; its disadvantage in sometimes creating a withdrawn observer of life rather than an intimate participant in it. Whitman's struggle between these two positions creates the drama of his reprise-poems.

In the case of Dickinson, I observe the way thinking can be continued through, and processed by means of, a repeating series. To this end, I examine in Dickinson's poetry a single template—the short narrative "plot"—as it appears in various modulations. I assume that the narrative structure of a poem testifies to the thinking (and feeling) antecedent to its expression, and I contrast Dickinson's "ideal" temporal structure (a serial step-by-step progress) with the abrupt and even chaotic rearrangements of temporal sequence that she is forced to invent in order to be faithful to her developing perception of what life's "plots" have actually turned out to be.

Finally, in the case of Yeats, I look at the way a poet can pursue the process of thinking by substituting for a second-order philosophical argument a montage of first-order images which supplement, or in some cases replace altogether, discursive statement. The mistrust of propositional statement as the sole means of intellectual accuracy reaches its height in some late poems of Yeats, in which identity itself is conceived as process, and a succession of images becomes the only way to disclose the truths, temporary and permanent alike, of identity.

There is nothing especially significant about the choice of cases here. My question—by what means does a poet reproduce an individual and characteristic process of thinking?—can be addressed to any work. I wanted, in planning the lectures which occasioned this book, to exemplify styles of poetic thinking that resort to various means: parody, reprise, serial sequence, and images. I also wanted to choose cases from a fairly long span of time, and to include examples from England, the United States, and Ireland. I ruled out, as cases, those poets who seem especially "philosophical" (Donne, Eliot, Stevens), because to discuss their relation to thinking would require an argument different from the one I am pursuing here: it would require distinguishing the nature of ruminative meditations in verse from ruminative meditations in prose.[4] Although it is self-evident that no philosopher ever wrote like Pope, it is possible to align the more reflective writings of Donne (the *Anniversaries*), Eliot *(Four Quartets),* or Stevens ("Sunday Morning") with certain fashions of religious or philosophical expression (scholastic philosophy, Anglican theology, Santayana's essays). Such parallels may illuminate the absorptive consciousness "behind" the poems, but the aesthetic specificity of each poem tends to disappear under the pressure of arguing for a common ideology. I have encountered this problem most disturbingly in reading philosophically oriented work on Stevens, in which the invoked philosophical parallels tend to suffocate the poet's aesthetic originality. I decided, therefore, to take as examples of lyric thinking forms of poetic discourse that could not possibly be closely analogized to the discourse of philosophical thought.

In poems, thinking is made visible not only to instruct but also to delight; it must enter somehow into the imaginative and linguistic fusion engaged in by the poem. While retaining its fierce intelligence, poetic thinking must not unbalance the poem in the direction of "thought." Yeats said (in "The Phases of the Moon") that at the aesthetic moment "all thought becomes an image," reminding us that poetry abstracts "reality"—including the reality of human thinking—into symbolic forms. The image itself, as both the product of thought and the bearer of thought, becomes thought made visible. Pope's spider feeling along the line, Whitman's spider sending out filaments, Dickinson's inventive night-spider ("A spider sewed at night"), Frost's albino spider ("Design") are not so much natural phenomena as images embodying thought. It is not enough to say that they are "emblems" with an allegorical "meaning": such labeling removes them from their participation in the ongoing thought-process which, as it produces the poem, summons them forth. By embedding such "emblems" in the intellectual and emotional turbulence within which they originate and which they help to clarify, I hope to establish poets as people who are *always* thinking, who create texts that embody elaborate and finely precise (and essentially unending) meditation. From the "Carbonates" that poets leave behind, we can deduce, as Dickinson asserts, the "fire [that] was," a fire as intellectual in its light as it is passionate in its heat.

1

Alexander Pope Thinking

MINIATURIZING, MODELING,
AND MOCKING IDEAS

And now a bubble burst, and now a world.

Essay on Man, I, 90

Poor guiltless I! and can I choose but smile,
When every coxcomb knows me by my style?

Epistle to Dr. Arbuthnot, 281–282

MY CONCERN with the relation of poetry to thinking in Alexander Pope originated from my indignation in the wake of a scholarly discussion. In 1983, feeling the winds of interdisciplinarity blowing, the Supervisors of the English Institute (a small yearly conference held at Harvard University) decided that it would be interesting to ask some practitioners of disciplines other than literature to discuss a single literary work. The text chosen was Alexander Pope's *An Essay on Man,*[1] a "philosophical" poem thought to be of a kind to interest scholars who often wrote about literary texts without being themselves "in English." The panel was called, according to the archives of the English Institute, "Then What Is Mankind's Proper Discipline?" A Harvard philosopher, a Harvard political scientist, and a non-Harvard anthropologist agreed to read the *Essay on Man* and comment on it.[2]

I listened, in the audience, as each of these scholars in turn dismissed the poem as of no contemporary interest. The philosopher regarded the poem as one enshrining an Enlightenment optimism that (certainly in the light of our present evaluation of human affairs) could no longer be endorsed by anyone: who, now, could subscribe to the idea that "Whatever is, is right"? The political scientist took up the social hierarchies described in the poem, as well as the idea that an equal happiness was given by God to all ranks of men. Although she approved of Pope's critique of vice among the great, she said that his concession to the desirability of a fixed social hierarchy reflected a point of view no longer supportable in contemporary political philosophy. The anthropologist fastened on the appearance in the poem of the Great Chain of Being, alluding to its historical importance as a cultural idea, but deploring it as unscientific and, in the light of fossil evidence, just plain wrong, since there are so many gaps in evolutionary series.

The panelists ended, with a certain complacency, by concluding that we were wiser than Pope, and that poems such as the *Essay on Man*—no matter how celebrated their authors—must be relegated, as outmoded artifacts, to the museum of cultural attitudes. The scandal to me, in this series of remarks, was that the eminent philosopher, the veteran political scientist, and the celebrated anthropologist had only one way of thinking about a poem: they translated it into its conceptual paraphrase, and proceeded to dismiss the paraphrase on the grounds of intellectual irrelevance to modern thought. They could hardly be blamed, in one sense, for doing this; Pope himself had prefaced each of the four Epistles of the *Essay on Man* with a prose "Argument," presenting the Argument as the microcosm of the epistle to follow. The scholars on the panel had perceived that Maynard Mack, the modern editor of Pope's *Essay,* had devoted most of his annotation to philosophical sources of and analogues to the classical and contemporary cultural ideas summarized in Pope's Arguments and reappearing in the succeeding Epistles; they followed Mack's lead in seeing the *Essay* as a series of ideas proposed by Pope as interesting and valuable ones.[3]

At the end of this interdisciplinary dismissal of the *Essay on Man,*

I felt pained on Pope's behalf. I did remark, in the subsequent discussion from the floor, that if Pope in his day had wanted to be considered a philosopher, he would not have written the *Essay* in verse. But I was not prepared to say, at that moment, what happens to culturally received "ideas" when they are reinvented in metrical and symbolic form. "Ideas" undergo peculiar stresses when they are incorporated into powerful poetry, and poets writing what we call "philosophical" verse are well aware of the degree to which, once domesticated in the topologically flexible bed of poetry, "ideas" are bent into peculiar shapes. (I resort to the unsatisfactory term "ideas" because it is the one commonly used. There is really, historically speaking, no such thing as an abstract "idea" except in mathematics; each "idea" is embedded in the tangle of its contemporary terms and occasions, and it is precisely that tangle that gives the poet his opportunity to make something odd and interesting out of any idea he touches.)

Representations of "ideas" in poetry are mischievously parasitic on the social situations in which, and the rhetoric by which, ideas are formally expressed in life. The social situations range from the loftiest—the printing of an essay by a serious philosopher—down to the most banal—the sermon by the ungifted homilist or the construction of a moral pamphlet for the education of the young. The rhetorical forms used for the presentation of ideas include such genres as the catechism, the Platonic dialogue, the philosophical axiom, the scholastic question-and-refutation, and so on. Speakers purveying "ideas" employ a series of well-known rhetorical strategies, from the Socratic hectoring question to the *pensée,* from the homely exemplum of the preacher to the *O altitudo* of the mystic. Whereas the rhetoric of the "true" philosopher, homilist, catechist, logician, or mystic will be directed chiefly by the serious and self-forgetful intent of his teaching, the poet, deep in the games of language, will be directed not only by his desire for exposition, but also by what intellectual brilliance he can evoke from playing with ideas: miniaturizing them, modeling them, mocking them.

The poet's acute self-consciousness with respect to language-games, generic thought-forms, and subliterary genres of exposition (the dialogue, the sermon) means that rhetorical strategies and social expository situations are to him, at every moment, available toys. He does not set his course from the philosophers; he does not follow a solely intellectual or catechetical intent. As Pope himself says, "A mutual commerce makes poetry flourish; but then Poets like Merchants, shou'd repay with something of their own what they take from others."[4] In Pope's hands, every didactic genre, every philosophical symbol, every expository social situation, every rhetorical scheme becomes first (given the brevity of poetry) miniaturized, and second, by that very miniaturization, parodied. I want to begin by giving some brief examples from Pope of this parodic representation of "ideas," which we are expected, being literary readers of a literary work, to recognize and be amused by. Pope makes much, for instance, in the *Essay on Man* of the sermonic form of direct address, which critics have referred to—not recognizing it in Pope as mild poetic parody—as "aggressive" or "hectoring." Of course it is hectoring; churchgoers have been hectored from the pulpit every Sunday. Of course it is aggressive; the homilist speaks with the certainty of divine revelation. But once transferred into a secular poem, that direct homiletic address rings with an absurd echo of its origins. Pope begins,

> Presumptuous Man! The reason wouldst thou find,
> Why formed so weak, so little, and so blind?
> [I, 34–35][5]

So far, so good: the putative sermon-attitude is merely replicated, though in little. But Pope's speaker, instead of answering the question as a preacher might—"So that thou wouldst learn thy dependence on thy Maker"—puts a preposterous mirror-image question in play, so that the whole passage reads:

> Presumptuous Man! The reason wouldst thou find,
> Why formed so weak, so little, and so blind?
> First, if thou canst, the harder reason guess,
> Why formed no weaker, blinder, and no less?[6]
>
> [I, 34–37]

As soon as the torsion of the mirror-question (one improbable in homily) is created, surface becomes emphasized at least equally with content, and an element of farce, inconsistent with true homily, is produced. The Popean idea of a "plain reason" is far from one that might convince a logician:

> Why has not Man a microscopic eye?
> For this plain reason, Man is not a Fly.
>
> [I, 193–194]

We are here very close—as indeed we are during much of the *Essay on Man*—to the Mad Hatter's tea party. Alice is often given "plain reasons" of this sort by the insistent logicians of Lewis Carroll's fantasy.

A further example of Pope's parodic rewriting of philosophical "ideas" may be seen as we continue to examine the passage beginning with the fly. Pope, being a poet—and not merely a philosopher—is joyfully inspired by the opportunities for whimsicality offered him by the invariant grids of the philosophers. There are, for instance, the five senses—sight, touch, smell, hearing, and taste. Once having started on an inventory of these five, a philosopher could scarcely be so cavalier as to omit one. But Pope's aim is not to *be* exhaustive, it is to give the *appearance* of exhaustiveness, for which four senses will do very well, since nobody, in a poem, is counting. The passage defending the putative adequacy of our sense-equipment, beginning with the mock-triumphant *q.e.d.* "Man is not a Fly," continues by illustrating how badly off we would be if all our senses were overdeveloped—a point easily made, if the intent were purely an intellectual one. But Pope's in-tent—as some commentators have indeed recognized—is to enact the experience of what it would be like to possess overdeveloped senses. In philosophical discussion since Plato and Aristotle, it is usual to treat first the "higher" senses, sight and hearing; Pope, un-conventionally, and upsetting the hierarchy, lists the senses as sight, touch, smell, and hearing. A logician might have given equal time to each of the four senses enumerated; Pope, being a logician of verse, finds it more amusing to create a chiasmus in the bestowing of proportion: while the first and last senses (sight and hearing) are awarded four lines each, the two middle ones (touch and smell) re-ceive only two, creating the pleasing "pre-arrangement" of 4:2:2:4. By giving sight and hearing the greater proportion of lines, and by making one the opening item, the other the closing item, on his list, Pope reminds us, in his own wayward way, of the convention-ally higher philosophical status of these two "theoretical" senses:

> Why has not Man a microscopic eye?
> For this plain reason, Man is not a Fly.
> Say what the use, were finer optics giv'n,
> T'inspect a mite, not comprehend the heav'n?
> Or touch, if trembling alive all o'er,
> To smart and agonize at ev'ry pore?
> Or quick effluvia darting thro' the brain,
> Die of a rose in aromatic pain?
> If nature thunder'd in his op'ning ears,
> And stunned him with the music of the spheres,[7]
> How would he wish that Heav'n had left him still
> The whisp'ring Zephyr, and the purling rill?
>
> [I, 193–204]

Such a passage is certainly not devoid of "ideas"—of "philosophi-cal" (or as we would now say, physiological) speculation. It points to the peculiar, and anciently noted, absence of a specific organ for touch (nothing comparable to the eye, the ear, the nose—how does touch function all over the body?); it reports the scientific notion that smells come to us via "effluvia" from their origin; and it refers to the medical idea of pain as the intensification of an otherwise normal sense-experience, rather as deafness can be the consequence of hearing a sound not proportioned to our ears. Nevertheless, none of these received ideas would be retailed in Pope's manner by a physiologist intent on describing the senses; his diction would remain more chaste, as in the summarizing note on Pliny by one of Pope's earliest commentators, Gilbert Wakefield, in his 1796 *Observations on Pope*: "Pliny fables of an ancient people, who subsisted by the smell of flowers only, and aromatic plants; and were deprived of life by the more violent effluvia of their odours."[8] Pliny himself says, tepidly enough (in Philemon Holland's translation), only that "Megasthenes [tells of] the Astomes [that] they . . . live only by the air, and smelling to sweet odours; no meat nor drink they take, only pleasant savours from divers and sundry roots, flowers, and wild fruits growing in the woods they entertain. . . . And yet if the scent be anything strong and stinking, they are soon therewith overcome, and die withal."[9] Pope, by contrast, cannot resist emphatic active verbals such as "trembling," "smart," "agonize," "darting," "pain," and "stun"—even while preserving, in such words as "use," "optics," "inspect," "comprehend," "effluvia," and "brain," a simulacrum of philosophical discourse.

If parody by simulacra of received discourses and common rhetorical moves, miniaturization of argument, re-schematizing (four senses in lieu of five), and lexical vivifying of sober expository sources are some of the things that happen to ideas when they are brought into the force-field of verse, what becomes of their status as ideas? They retain that status, to some degree—that is, we can observe which received ideas from his culture Pope decided to include in his *Essay*—but the very nature of his verse tells us that he holds all such ideas, for the purpose of the poem, only provisionally. Pope can present ideas genuinely, even didactically—since poets tend to believe what they take the trouble to write down and present to others—but he does not attempt to impose them on his readers. Instead, ideas—such as those on the adequacy of our senses—are framed, posed, choreographed, heightened, and refined or coarsened. They are recommended as wonderful artifacts of human mentality, apt for exhibition, rather than as guides for life or as philosophical axioms.

In taking up a philosophical "idea," then—such as man's susceptibility to vice—Pope, unlike a genuine homilist, is often ready to end a passage with a sort of worldly shrug. It is at such moments that he reminds us most of Montaigne, one of his favorite authors; but even Montaigne does not have the absurdity (in expository terms) of verse shimmering over his ironic play of thought. Pope begins with a sentence that might not be out of place in a sermon:

> Vice is a monster of so frightful mien,
> As, to be hated, needs but to be seen.
> [II, 217–218]

No statement could be more unequivocal, more apparently serious. And yet, hear how Pope continues:

> Vice is a monster of so frightful mien,
> As, to be hated, needs but to be seen;
> Yet seen too oft, familiar with her face,
> We first endure, then pity, then embrace.
> But where th'Extreme of Vice, was ne'er agreed:
> Ask where's the North? At York, 'tis on the Tweed;
> In Scotland at the Orcades; and there,
> At Greenland, Zembla, or the Lord knows where.
> [II, 217–224]

This passage on the "monster," Vice, which brings us, not slowly, into her embrace, and which, in discussing the location of "th'Extreme of Vice," falls into mention of the Tweed and the Orkneys, only to end with a throwing up of hands—"the Lord knows where"—is a gleeful parody of Spenserian allegory, homiletic diction, and geographic parochiality.

I need to concede, at this point, that not all of the *Essay* is parodic or satiric to this degree. Yet, to my ear, it is all parodic of the treatise form. In the eighteenth century, serious philosophical or religious exposition was normally done in prose. It is Hobbes and Shaftesbury and Locke that Pope's commentators cite; and if they turn to Dryden's *Religio Laici*—a more earnest poem than Pope's—it is to emphasize how different its coherent logical texture is from that of Pope's *Essay*.[10]

What happens, then, to "ideas" brought within the magnetic force of Pope's verse when they are *not* being overtly parodied, miniaturized, sensualized, re-schematized, or capriciously dismissed? They are subdued to the second commandment of the good poet: "Thou shalt not be boring." (The first commandment is "Thou shalt imagine.") Let me offer an example. In wishing to depict an original Golden Age, in which "The state of Nature was the reign of God," Pope borrows from the conventional descriptions of the prelapsarian age when man was a vegetarian and lived in harmony with the beasts, when religion was universal, and when social rule was compassionate. He follows convention, too, in wishing to show how far man has now fallen from this state. The received way of showing the fall was to describe, in glowing terms, the original harmony of man and nature, and then, by contrast, to lament the savagery into which the social world subsequently declined. This linear process of the good becoming the bad is the procedure, one notes, of all the parallel passages quoted in the Twickenham edition of the *Essay*. Pope indeed begins, like his precursors, with an evocation of original harmony, but into the middle of his exposition he slips a line about the absence of some vices which occur only in postlapsarian time: "Pride then was not; nor Arts, that Pride to aid." The blandness, negation, and abstraction of this line prevent its causing much disturbance to prelapsarian harmony, however, and the original benevolent social state immediately, and reassuringly, returns:

> Nor think, in NATURE'S STATE they blindly trod;
> The state of Nature was the reign of God:
> Self-love and Social at her birth began,
> Union the bond of all things, and of Man.
> Pride then was not; nor Arts, that Pride to aid;
> Man walked with beast, joint tenant of the shade;
> The same his table, and the same his bed.
> [III, 147–153]

After a subsequent single line's interruption—to which I will return—the picture of the Golden Age continues, reiterating, in the phrase "the same" (used of religion) the continuing harmony of man and beast:

> In the same temple, the resounding wood,
> All vocal beings hymn'd their equal God.
> [III, 155–156]

However, by inserting line 154, in contrastive mood, between these two placid moments, Pope spills gore (if only in negation) on the Golden Age. Over his prelapsarian era, the poet casts his knowledge of the bloody future, when unnatural man will begin to slaughter animals for fur and food:

> Man walked with beast, joint tenant of the shade;
> The same his table, and the same his bed;
> No murder cloathed him, and no murder fed.
> In the same temple, the resounding wood,
> All vocal beings hymn'd their equal God.
> [III, 152–156]

The staged "attempt"—after the violent double intrusion of the word "murder"—to "revert" to a "pure" non-contrastive description of religion in lines 155–156 immediately meets with dramatic resistance in the next, contrastive, definition of vegetarian religion, which practiced the sacrifice of inanimate objects rather than of beasts. By comparison with his earlier inoffensive observations about the absence of Pride and the Arts, Pope's new negations are a tour de force describing original good through later bad:

> All vocal beings hymn'd their equal God:
> The shrine with gore unstain'd, with gold undrest,
> Unbrib'd, unbloody, stood the blameless priest.
>   [III, 156–158]

This well-known poetic technique of double exposure—in which the innocent prelapsarian shrine is proleptically stained with gore and dressed with gold, the blameless priest proleptically corrupted by bribes and bloodied by his hecatombs or his religious wars—is introduced for a purpose. Aware that his readers already know the myth of the Golden Age, Pope diverts himself by retailing that topic "innocently" at first, but subversively and sinisterly at last. It is not that Pope disavows the "idea" of an original harmonious state of nature; he genuinely presents it, as an artist who certainly prefers that myth to the darker Hobbesian conjecture. But we can see, by his insistent use of prolepsis, that Pope thinks that the Golden Age is something we conceive of only by a back-formation from our actual stained, bribed, murderous, and bloody present. He will not allow the conventional philosophical preservation of the sentimental prelapsarian idyll by sequestering it from its criminal sequel. We can "believe" in the "idea" of the Golden Age only if we admit it to be a nostalgic myth confected from our fallen present. If we were to discuss Pope's "thinking" in this passage, we would describe it as an insight into the social construction of original idylls.

I believe the same sophisticated reframing can be demonstrated in Pope's exhibition of other received "ideas." He was, for example, far too satiric in temper and far too worldly in experience to think that "ideas" exist in a chaste realm protected from actuality. He therefore constantly coarsens his discourse, letting it fall from the philosophical to the actual. In prefacing Epistle IV, in which he will discuss the nature of happiness, he asserts blandly, in the prose Argument, Part VI:

> That *external goods* are not the proper rewards, but often inconsistent with, or destructive of Virtue. That even these can make no Man happy without Virtue: Instanced in *Riches; Honours; Nobility; Greatness; Fame; Superior Talents*. With pictures of human Infelicity in Men possessed of them all.

Sometimes one feels that commentators on the *Essay on Man* have been reading only Pope's Arguments, and not the poem—because when we look to the poem to find these instances, these pictures, of the possession of external goods "inconsistent with, or destructive of Virtue," we find Pope abandoning the lofty discourse of the Argument for these coarse lines of exemplification:

> To sigh for ribbands if thou art so silly,
> Mark how they grace Lord Umbra, or Sir Billy:
> Is yellow dirt the passion of thy life?
> Look but on Gripus, or on Gripus' wife:
> If Parts allure thee, think how Bacon shined,
> The wisest, brightest, meanest of mankind:
> Or ravished with the whistling of a Name,
> See Cromwell, damned to everlasting fame!
>   [IV, 277–284]

Critics normally account for such a passage by remarking that Pope is a "satirist." Yes—but what does "being a satirist" mean in the exposition of "ideas" (such as this one, that infelicity attends the non-virtuous man even if he is rich in worldly goods)? And how seriously are we to take the gay exempla of ribbons and yellow dirt in our response to this idea? And how adequate to "real" history are Pope's cartoons of Bacon and Cromwell? We find ourselves in the realm of caricature, where a single characteristic—Bacon's meanness—is exaggerated like a Daumier paunch. Expositors of ideas about virtue and vice can hardly afford to be witty caricaturists if they are in earnest; and though cartoonists may be prompted by "ideas," they are not expositors of them except in that lightning flash of exposure proper to cartoons. If we were to discuss Pope's "thinking" here, it might be to describe the one-stroke strategies he invents for making exempla into caricature: synecdoche (the effeminate ribbons for the acts of civic virtue they symbolize); nickname ("Sir Billy"); scientific reduction (by which gold is merely "yellow dirt"); classical allusion ("Gripus"); anticlimax ("wisest, brightest, *meanest*"); word-substitution ("damned to everlasting [condemnation] fame"). Each of these strategies represents an act of thought about the art of caricature, and how it may be accomplished: or, to put it more truly, each draws, instinctually, on Pope's huge and learned reservoir of strategic diminution. In responding afresh to each line of satiric jeering, the reader—"ravished with the whistling of" the names of Lord Umbra, Sir Billy, Gripus, Bacon, and Cromwell—has forgotten that he is receiving a lesson in the discordance of external riches and internal virtue. The idea has been sidelined by the poet's delight in his exempla.

If we bracket, in viewing the *Essay on Man,* the vivid image, the satiric sally, the deformation of expository genres, the parodic rhetoric, the miniaturized logic—and the attempt above all not to be long-winded—and ask, beyond these, what else makes the *Essay* so odd, we can see that one of Pope's chief poetic principles, that of syntactic variety, continually "distorts" his expression of "ideas," tugging his pen away from normal syntactic procedures of exposition. We have seen one example of peculiar syntactic *non*-variety— itself conspicuous—in the mirror-image repeating the question representing man as little, weak, and blind. Deliberate *non*-mirror-

images are as strange and noticeable a phenomenon as are deliber-
ate mirror-images. Normally, syntactic parallels ought to resemble
each other; and Pope knows very well how to create a standard
rhetorical parallel. "I showed," he says in concluding his poem,

> THAT REASON, PASSION, answer one great aim;
> That true SELF-LOVE and SOCIAL are the same;
> That VIRTUE only makes our Bliss below;
> And all our Knowledge is, OURSELVES TO KNOW.
> [IV, 395–398]

Here, each clause is alike, and we read them, intellectually, as paral-
lel instances of what Pope has "showed."[11] In spite of small individ-
ual differences, the parallels are strong enough to make the passage
stand foursquare, each line a separate noun clause recapitulating
something demonstrated.

We might compare, to this standard and lucid form of parallel
construction, another far more trickily devised. In Epistle I, Pope
has just declared that "'Tis but a part we see, and not a whole."
The exemplification of the axiom follows, to prove that we cannot
understand Fate's handling of us any more than domestic beasts
can understand our handling of them. Pope sets in parallel a horse,
an ox, and man. The horse, as used by man, has two announced
potentials, and they are logical opposites: the animal may be re-
strained, or he may be driven. The ox, as used by man, has three
potentials, which exist in no such logical relation: the ox may break
the clod as a domesticated animal; or he may become a sacrificial
victim; or he might be (as in Egypt) worshipped as a god. At first,
the clichéd adjectives denominating the beasts seem incidental; we
hear of the "proud" steed and the "dull" ox:

> When the proud steed shall know why Man restrains
> His fiery course, or drives him o'er the plains;
> When the dull Ox, why now he breaks the clod,
> Is now a victim, and now Egypt's God:

Then shall Man's pride and dulness comprehend
His actions', passions', being's, use and end.
     [I, 61–66]

"Yes," we say, "I now see that Man fails to comprehend his state either because of pride or because of dullness, and those two vices account for the choice of the horse and the ox, the one to bring pride before us, the other to make us see what Pope means by dullness." But to say that the horse can't find a reason for man's opposite commands to drive or restrain, or the ox understand its odd threefold fates, and then to rise from these, in line 66, to a *compte rendu* of all the actions and passions and being of man, their functional use and philosophical end, is to make a preposterously large jump, and to offer entirely too many parallels at once. We object to this flurry of signification, but "Wait," replies the poet, "I have scarcely begun," and adds,

Why, doing, suffering, checked, impelled; and why
This hour a slave, the next a deity.
     [I, 67–68]

"Yes," we reply, "I do see that *doing* goes with *actions'* and *suffering* with *passions'*, but—oh yes, *checked* goes with *restrains* and *impelled* with *drives* (we are back to the horse), and *slave* goes with *victim*, and *deity* with *God* (we are back to the ox)." But was it quite necessary, for clarity of exposition, to tack on, in lines 67–68, a two-line ledger-entry summing up the previous six lines? Normally, once a parallel has been completed—and this one is complete by line 66— we leave it there on the page; we don't recapitulate it at one-third its former length. No one intent on philosophical lucidity in the exposition of ideas would explain, using fiendishly compressed syntax of this sort, the simple received idea that man does not understand his fate at the hand of God any more than animals do theirs at the hand of man.

What, then, is impelling the poet here to these syntactic heapings, making these lines so different from the clear offering of the idea in the Argument: "That Man is . . . conformable to *Ends* and *Relations* to him unknown"? It seems that once Pope has put on his heroic couplets, something very peculiar happens to exposition. The Muse, who scorns such unvivacious abstract language as that composing the Argument, commands: *Find the exempla.* And so the poet does, just as a homilist would do: the horse and the ox. But to make the exposition interestingly unsettled to the mind, the horse is given a logical binary possibility for its ends, the ox an alogical ternary one. The Muse then utters a second challenge: *Make it concise.* And so the poet crams into two lines Man's pride and dullness and actions and passions and being, their use and their end. Who could want more? But the Muse presses further: *Shorter,* she says, flogging her poet as man flogs the beasts. And the rapid parallels become mummified in a single summary model—still more rapid and more confusing—which skewers us, in its compressed conflation, to horse and ox, actions and passions, victims and gods.[12]

Pope was no doubt confident that he was exemplifying his Argument; but he was more truly engaged in finding—in this contorted model-shrinking—language that made him delighted with himself as he implicitly critiqued the "boring" procedures of the standard exposition of ideas. What delights the poet, then, in the exposition of an idea? I am afraid the answer is "quasi-unintelligibility," together with the two answers Pope gave (in the "Design" prefacing the *Essay*)—memorableness and concision. "[This essay forms]," he wrote, "a temperate yet not inconsistent, and a short yet not imperfect system of Ethics." And, in answer to an obvious objection—that a philosophical system should be expressed in prose—he adds:

> This I might have done in prose; but I chose verse, and even rhyme, for two reasons. The one will appear obvious; that principles, maxims, or precepts so written, both strike the

reader more strongly at first, and are more easily retained by him afterwards: The other may seem odd, but is true, I found I could express them more *shortly* this way than in prose itself; and nothing is more certain, than that much of the *force* as well as *grace* of arguments or instructions, depends on their *conciseness*. I was unable to treat this part of my subject more in *detail*, without becoming dry and tedious, or more *poetically*, without sacrificing perspicuity to ornament, without wandering from the precision, or breaking the chain of reasoning. If any man can unite all these without diminution of any of them, I freely confess he will compass a thing above my capacity.

One believes Pope's statement: he wanted to find force and grace, a balance between tedium (creating a poem too detailed, too prosy) and over-ornamentation (creating a poem too fantastic, too "poetic," too "imprecise"). And yet, when I say that what delights the poet is "unintelligibility," I mean to point to those passages in which language doesn't sound like anything anyone could possibly say either in "real life" or in "real philosophy." The disquisition on the horse and ox is such a passage. To read it aloud is almost inevitably to stumble—in intonation, emphasis, or enunciation—at lines six and seven in the attempt to connect them tonally, all at once, with the horse and ox and man—"His actions', passions', being's, use and end; / Why, doing, suffering, checked, impelled; and why—." The effect is that of a grammatical surfeit of indigestible words—first all nouns, then all verbs—rather than that of a meaningful conceptual utterance, or an utterance aiming to enlighten a reader.

There are many other such passages in Pope, all of them witty and spirited. In them, language is shown to be faster, more congested, more complex, more witty, more grammatically heaped, than the "ideas"—so simple, so baldly statable in the Argument—

to which words are conventionally thought to be subordinate. Such a passage displays the poet's revenge on the moribund encapsulation of received "ideas" and on the characteristically flat rhetoric by which they are expounded. If we investigate Pope's thinking as we perceive it through such a passage, we find that it is not occupied with the putatively purveyed idea of man's inability to interpret his fate, but rather with a mocking demonstration that most philosophical arguments in prose are simply too drearily long, and, with a little effort, could be profitably condensed into a run of some dozen words. (Such a reflection consorts well with Pope's praise of Montaigne's electricity, vivacities, and volatilities.)[13]

If, then, it is not so much ideas that Pope is after as the representation of his own more vivid form of thinking, how shall we define the kind of thinking that the literary reader finds in Pope? It is a thinking—to use Pope's own formulation—that is driven toward concision and memorableness, one that loves showy ornament but equally loves precision. As leaden "ideas" rephrase themselves in his witty and exquisitely literary brain, Pope creates a cinematic flow of living thought, instead of presenting—as his Arguments do—thought embalmed. Living thought must establish itself as the norm at the very beginning of the verse (if only to counteract the prose thicket of the "Design" and "Argument" through which the patient reader has already struggled). Living thought has to be quick and mobile, ever darting to extremes and polarities, but resting in none of them. Living thought must, like ordinary thought, characterize, allegorize, reason, denominate, and analogize—but it must also jump up and down, over and under, left and right; it must swell and contract, leap from register to register, joke and feel pangs. Above all, it must advance too swiftly for instant intelligibility: the reader must hang on for the ride, bouncing to the next hurdle hardly having recovered his seat from the last. It is as if the poet wants to say, "This is what thinking really is like: have you ever known it?"

And so Pope, constructing the wonderful and deservedly famous overture to his second Epistle, fully conscious that he is competing with the Oracle of Delphi, the Bible, and *Hamlet*, opens briskly,

> Know then thyself, presume not God to scan,
> The proper study of Mankind is Man.
> [II, 1–2][14]

After this initiating adjuration—so energetically and usefully relegating theology to the realm of the impossible—Pope goes on to create Man. The creation passage—a single sentence—is characteristically Popean in moving from structure to structure, rendering graphically the mobility of mind as it operates at full tilt. Let me say a little about this self-description of—for so I see it—Pope by Pope. Detached from all reference to his own biography, Pope is not, here, the warm friend, the social companion, the scourge of dullards, or the pious son; rather, he is looking at himself in his interior solitude. Before his eyes, in a secular *Ecce Homo*, he places himself: the strange genius-cripple, the frustrated yearner, the inquisitive skeptic, the Catholic deist, the gothic classicist, the ill sensualist, the self-deluding self-satirist, the baffled inquirer, the language-tethered visionary. He is bold enough to think that what he sees in himself can be generalized to the rest of us, as he describes archetypal Man:

> Placed on this isthmus of a middle state,
> A Being darkly wise, and rudely great:
> With too much knowledge for the Sceptic side,
> With too much weakness for the Stoic's pride,
> He hangs between; in doubt to act, or rest;
> In doubt to deem himself a God, or Beast;
> In doubt his Mind or Body to prefer;
> Born but to die, and reasoning but to err;
> Alike in ignorance, his reason such,

Whether he thinks too little, or too much:
Chaos of Thought and Passion, all confused;
Still by himself abused, or disabused;
Created half to rise, and half to fall;
Great lord of all things, yet a prey to all;
Sole judge of Truth, in endless Error hurled:
The glory, jest, and riddle of the world!

[II, 3–18]

There is a magnificence and courage in these lines which Pope had reason to be proud of, but which we may not fully recognize unless we recall how bold Pope had to be in so correcting the received Christian image of man. No Christian would think that man might be in doubt whether to deem himself a God or a Beast. Still less would any Christian approve of a man who doubted whether to prefer his mind or his body, leaving his soul unmentioned. Nor would a Christian believe that man is born but to die: man, he would assert, is born to save his soul and live eternally. The Christian man would find it blasphemy to appoint himself the sole judge of truth. And to the ordinary Christian way of thinking, man is hardly a Pascalian jest; he is the image and likeness of God. Pope had been educated in Catholic schools; he remained loyal, even at the cost of social and political disadvantage, to his parents' religious affiliation; and yet the theological doctrines he had been taught concerning the nature of man are not those affirmed here. These are judgments—however ratified by Shaftesbury and later codified by Warburton—that he had taken to himself: the passage rings with a superb and personal conviction.

The chief assertion of this famous set piece is the middleness of man, as he "hangs between"; it is not usually acknowledged how uncomfortable a position is implied if "hanging between" is one's lifelong posture. While the mental equivalent of the physical "hanging between" is being "in doubt"—a phrase thrice repeated— the geometrical equivalent of "hanging between" is being divided in "half"—a phrase twice repeated, and prosodically enacted in the many lines divided by a medial caesura. The poles between which man hangs are quickly erected: Skepticism and Stoicism; action and repose; God and Beast; Mind and Body; birth and death; ignorance and knowledge; too little and too much; Thought and Passion; rising and falling; lord and prey; Truth and Error. These categories contrast, in very rapid succession, conventional philosophical terms and positions; the active versus the contemplative life; spiritual versus sensual life; mental versus physical life; the human *terminus a quo* and *terminus ad quem;* excess versus defect of knowledge; elevation versus depression of ontological status; governance versus subordination; the true and the false; knowing and not knowing. Not everything in the passage is so neatly binary, but for the most part Pope characterizes life and thinking as trapeze acts in which one swings, or is swung, from one extreme to another, hardly ever, if ever, at rest. "The man whose mind was made up, and who, therefore, died"—Wallace Stevens's image of the man who is the antithesis of the poet—is the negative of Pope's self-portrait. This is why it seems to me so unjust that Pope should be described—even by some of his most devoted scholars—as an expositor of received ideas. His only "system" is to find himself constantly "hurled" and "hanging": he, like his God, sees "Atoms or systems into ruin hurled, / And now a bubble burst, and now a world" [I, 89–90].

The non-binary moments anchoring this great sentence of opposing positions come both early and late. The first non-binary is the stable geographic image by which man is "placed" on "this isthmus of a middle state." When—rarely—Pope allows himself to be at rest on solid ground, he is aware of vast continents or oceans of the unexplored on both left and right. In such figures of geographic immobility, the inherent doubleness of existence is displaced onto the vistas extending to the left and right. Only once more in the passage does Pope stand still, in the blazoned epithets with which the sentence ends, where man, exhibited for the first time in a social context, is named "The glory, jest, and riddle of the world." Here man is not made a concept-divided-in-two, as before. The three nouns appear as freestanding radial aspects of man rather than qualities related by opposition to each other. Against the backdrop of the world, which grounds these epithets concerning man, Pope offers three conjectures. *Glory* is a religious word; man is God. *Jest* is a social word; man is an actor in the farce observed by the gods. *Riddle* is an intellectual word; man is inexhaustible to the inquiry of the mind. The objectivity of this sudden stationing of man—after the troubled interiority of such phrases as "in doubt" and "hang[ing] between" and "think[ing] too little or too much"—is a triumph of detachment. It is as though an idiosyncratic self-portrait were to suddenly geometrize itself into Vitruvian archetype.

Let me now say a word about the rhythms of Pope's thinking.[15] When we note the syllables at which caesuras appear in the lines on man that open Epistle II, the record looks like this:

4–6	Know then thyself,// presume not God to scan;
10	The proper study of Mankind is Man.
10	Placed on this isthmus of a middle state,
6–4	A Being darkly wise,// and rudely great:
10	With too much knowledge for the Sceptic side,
10	With too much weakness for the Stoic's pride,
4–4–2	He hangs between:// in doubt to act,// or rest;
8–2	In doubt to deem himself a God,// or Beast;
10	In doubt his Mind or Body to prefer;
4–6	Born but to die,// and reasoning but to err;
6–4	Alike in ignorance,// his reason such,
7–3	Whether he thinks too little,// or too much:
7–3	Chaos of Thought and Passion,// all confused;
6–4	Still by himself abused,// or disabused;
6–4	Created half to rise,// and half to fall;

5–5	Great lord of all things,// yet a prey to all;
4–6	Sole judge of Truth,// in endless Error hurled:
3–1–6	The glory,// jest,// and riddle of the world!

The breadth of the "middle state" generates the lines without cae-
suras, while the "doubleness" of man's doubt generates the lines
that keep breaking into two halves. (Pope thereby shows us the
"contamination" of the rhythm of thinking by what is being
thought about.) The opening couplet of the passage exhibits both
patterns: first, the "split" pattern contrasting the propriety of self-
investigation with the impropriety of theological pursuits ("Know
then thyself,// presume not God to scan"); and second, the broad
unbroken decasyllabic "isthmus" pattern placing us on solid
ground ("The proper study of Mankind is Man"). The most prob-
lematic "isthmus" line is one which "ought," given its semantic
content, to break into two: "In doubt his Mind or Body to prefer."
Perhaps it is broad rather than split because it serves as the last
bridge from the "isthmus" condition to the "broken" condition,
which prevails for the rest of the passage. In the interesting line "A
Being darkly wise, and rudely great," Pope allows us, twice, to see
man's nature in its original oxymoronic chaos of opposites before
the elements have begun to "choose sides," analytically speaking.
Had this notion occurred later in the passage, such qualities would
have already "separated out" from chaos to their polar extremes,
and the line would have had to read "Dark in his wisdom,// and in
rudeness great." For a moment, however, in this formulation by ad-
verbial paradox ("darkly wise"), we are permitted to see man's op-
posing qualities physiologically *in situ,* before the analytic intellect
portions them out into permanent antitheses. Each of Pope's syn-
tactic formulas in these lines shows a mind thinking how it might
frame a particular question: here, should the mixed nature of man
be formulated mixedly (adverbially) or laid out in categorical an-
titheses?

But it is not only by the metrical break of a caesura, or by adverbial paradox, that Pope makes us feel the opposing qualities of human nature. An unbroken half-line may often contain an internal semantic opposition, conferring on the whole line four, rather than two, semantic crests, creating a higher degree of "brokenness":

Born but to die, / / and reasoning but to err.

As Pope thinks about how man's internal antitheses actually manifest themselves in life, he demonstrates how they sometimes coexist ("*With* too much x, *with* too much y"); sometimes alternate ("in doubt to act, *or* rest"); sometimes add to each other ("Born but to die, *and* reasoning but to err"); and sometimes become adversative ("Great lord of all things, *yet* a prey to all"). These different formulations of the "same" binary condition keep us from sitting firmly in our saddle. The final line of the passage ("The glory, jest, and riddle of the world") where the two caesuras come at very odd metrical places (after the third *and* fourth syllables) tells us, by its meter as well as its language, that man is not merely isthmused, not merely split in half, not merely multifaceted, but—since the third term of the three, *riddle*, opens out to an indefinite number of aspects—uncompassable within any pre-existing formulas. Here we see thinking not quite giving up on thought, but certainly admitting the impossibility of conclusive analysis, or of a stable system.

   Is there an order to Pope's thinking as this passage evolves? The opening formulas borrow from the dualism of Pope's intellectual upbringing, whether physiological (mind or body), philosophical (Skeptic or Stoic), or vocational (to act, or rest). But such dualism vanishes when it is suggested (by the phrase "but to") that there exists an implicit Fate that dooms man to die and to err: he is "Born *but to* die, and reasoning *but to* err." Pope offers no hopeful dualism with respect to death ["Born but to die, and then to live again"]; nor is there any optimistic dualism with respect to reasoning ["Reasoning both to solve and then to err"]. There is no dualism, either,

as regards thinking: the outcome is the same ignorance, whether
man thinks too little or too much. These deviations into hopeless-
ness vitiate, for the moment, the earlier inquiring vacillation be-
tween philosophical or vocational choices. The neat caesural par-
titions by which opposition was expressed are now rebuked by
the caesura of identity: "Chaos of Thought and Passion,// all
confused." Chaos and Confusion are indistinguishable, and once
Thought and Passion have been confused into a Chaos, they can-
not be resolved into their separateness again. Similarly, the identity
of verbal root in the words *abused* and *disabused* suggests a cycle of
self-constituting dissolutions hardly to be distinguished in phase
since they are always in process; and where can we locate a body
that half rises and half falls, if not always in the same place? Yet in
the wake of early divisions and later despairs, Pope places at the
close of the passage the glorious epithets "Great lord of all things"
and "Sole judge of Truth." These place us in a different relation to
our subject, Man, so recently a "Chaos." Having cleared the decks
by saying the worst about man's division, confusion, and cycles of
abusing and disabusing, Pope allows light into the former darkness.
Who but man is lord of all things? Who but man can be the sole
judge of truth here on earth? It does not matter, really, that man is
also a prey, or that he is hurled—by the same Fate that dooms him
to death—into endless Error: he remains the glory, undisputed, of
the world—if also its jest and its riddle. It cannot have been easy
for the deformed and unpartnered Pope to see himself as a glory,
but I think we believe the assertion when it comes, given all the ag-
itated truth-telling that has preceded it. In its inclusion of division
and contrast, confusion and stasis, glory and mystery, this passage
reveals Pope to be a thinker who would rather embrace all con-
flicting human truths than expound any one subset of them.

How, then, does Pope, thinking, represent thought itself? As
something that tends to become systematized, yes; as something
that has been rhetorically expounded by a set of conventional strat-
egies, yes; as something widely shared, in symbols and in terminol-

ogy, within a given culture, yes. And the Arguments to the four
Epistles of the *Essay* say as much, in a flat and abstract form that
critics have been only too ready to sustain. But how else does the
Essay represent thought? As something that can be parodied, jested
with, coarsened, inhumanly speeded-up; something mobile in its
flickering, ever tumbling over into nonsense, smooth at times,
rough at times, serious and funny by turns, giddy and solemn, wit-
tily resourceful in its self-expression in language; something that
can always bring an edge to the mind and a smile to the lips. As
Pope said in a solemn moment, on the death of his mother, "All
our passions are Inconsistencies, and our very Reason is no better.
But we are what we were Made to be."[16] The joyful rapidity of the
Essay on Man makes me think that it was perhaps more delightful
to think in verse in Pope's age than it ever since has been; it is cer-
tain that no subsequent poet, except perhaps Auden, has leapt in
verse from conjecture to conjecture so unexpectedly and wittily
as he.

In the 1983 conference that I described at the beginning of this
chapter, Pope was superficially read and in consequence dismissed
as irrelevant. But perhaps the next philosopher to reflect on the *Es-
say on Man* will perceive in it not outworn systems but something
more complex: Pope's admission of man's need for the grids of
system but at the same time his demonstration of the instability
and insufficiency of all systems, whether scientific, legal, or ethi-
cal.[17] After all, the Angels "showed a NEWTON as we show an Ape"
[II, 34]; and within a legal system right can only too predictably
"harden into wrong" [III, 193]. On morals, too, there is no con-
sensus:

> The good must merit God's peculiar care;
> But who, but God, can tell us who they are?
> One thinks on Calvin Heaven's own spirit fell;
> Another deems him instrument of hell.
> [IV, 135–138]

The next anthropologist looking at the *Essay* might see not the pleasant aesthetic fiction of the Great Chain of Being, but rather Pope's savage renditions of the tribal customs of eighteenth-century society: "Stuck o'er with titles and hung round with strings, / That"—says Pope witheringly—"thou mayst be by kings, or whores of kings," encapsulating the privilege-system and the libidinousness of the court in one scathing anticlimax. And the next political scientist to read this poem might investigate in it not the remnants of a discredited social order but rather Pope's dismissal, at every moment, of the assumption that aristocracy and merit are one:

> Go! If your ancient, but ignoble blood
> Has crept through scoundrels ever since the flood,
> Go! And pretend your family is young;
> Nor own, your fathers have been fools so long.
> [IV, 211–214]

Readings by scholars from disciplines other than literature may still be content-driven, but at least they can acknowledge Pope's thinking as producing something more intelligent than outdated cultural detritus. Such future scholars may read Pope as a man no less acute in thinking about human affairs than themselves; and think him a poet more subtle about systems than their predecessors perceived him to be. Properly literary readings, alive to the electric flickers of Pope's language, ought to admit us even further to Pope's ceaselessly energetic and subversive forms of thinking.[18]

Walt Whitman Thinking

TRANSCRIPTION, REPRISE,
AND TEMPTATIONS RESISTED

The pure, extravagant, yearning, questioning artist's face.

Leaves of Grass (1855)[1]

We put a second brain to the brain,
We put second eyes to the eyes and second ears to the ears.

Early uncollected fragment[2]

Remember how many pass their whole lives and hardly once think
and never learned themselves to think,
Remember before all realities must exist their thoughts.[3]

WHEN AND HOW does thinking appear in the poetry of Walt Whitman? How are the perceptions received by his exuberant senses modified by intellectual and aesthetic activity? How will his language representing initial perception differ from his language representing perception-as-thought? Such questions are not often put to Whitman's works. I want to suggest that we can find out something about Whitman and his characteristic processes of thinking by considering his recourse to a single structural genre— that of the reprise. I give the genre this name (borrowing from its use in music) because its salient characteristic is the repetition-with-difference, in the second part of a poem, of a scene or incident appearing in the first part.

Whitman has never been granted much intellectual capacity. "It is as if the beasts spoke," said Thoreau in a letter to H. G. O. Blake, and Santayana was in accord. In Whitman, he said,

> We find the swarms of men and objects rendered as they might strike the retina in a sort of waking dream. It is the most sincere possible confession of the lowest—I mean the most primitive—type of perception. All ancient poets are so-phisticated in comparison and give proof of longer intellectual and moral training. Walt Whitman has gone back to the innocent style of Adam.[4]

Whitman was indeed interested in conveying "the most primitive type of perception." But into his ultimate rendition of that sort of perception he incorporated processes of thinking that, as I hope to show, went far beyond retinal innocence.

Although Whitman reinvents all the usual lyric genres—and we still lack adequate descriptions of his originality in this respect—the reprise, because its very core is self-revision, is particularly revealing of the infiltration (one could say) of perception by intellectuality throughout his work. In a reprise, perceptual transcription is supplemented by a second step, which one could call the interpretation or refocusing of the transcriptive. And there is a further reason to look at Whitman's poems of reprise. Reprise is, we could say, merely the enlargement, into a freestanding lyric lattice, of the basic molecule of Whitmanian chemistry, the semantic or syntactic parallel. The smallest parallels in Whitman come two to a line: "I celebrate myself, and sing myself." When the parallels grow more complex, each requires a whole line, and we come near to the psalmic parallel, so often imitated by Whitman, in which the second verse adds something to the substance of the first. But when parallels grow too large for a single line or a couplet, they begin to require at least a stanza apiece, generating the essentially binary poem of reprise, in which the second half redoes—but in an altered fashion—the first. Usually, in Whitman, the first, transcriptive, half presents initial perceptions, while the second half records perceptions into which thoughts have been almost invisibly incorporated. Because it shows us the "late" entrance of intellectual formulation into a Whitman lyric, the reprise-poem is a good place to observe how reflective thinking modifies Whitman's apparently "spontaneous" language and form. Because the second part of a reprise-poem generally resembles the first in incident and theme, the genre of reprise formally foregrounds style as that which distinguishes the two halves.

In examining three characteristic, but also significantly different, poems of reprise—"Sparkles from the Wheel," "A Noiseless Patient Spider," and "Come Up from the Fields Father"—I want to deduce from the surface of each lyric the kind of poetic thinking that the construction of reprise, in that instance, has required. I should mention parenthetically that many of Whitman's other lyrics are also structured by reprise: they include such famous short poems as "I Saw in Louisiana a Live-Oak Growing" (1860) and "Vigil Strange I Kept on the Field One Night" (1865), as well as "Earth, My Likeness" (1860) and "Hours Continuing Long" (1860).[5] Other poems, such as "These I Singing in Spring" (1860) and "As I Ebb'd with the Ocean of Life" (1860), use reprise for closure, without being fundamentally structured by it. Although Whitman's major sequences are of course too long to be structured by reprise alone, the closing section (9) of "Crossing Brooklyn Ferry" (1856) is an opulent reprise of the scenes earlier summoned; and "When Lilacs Last in the Dooryard Bloom'd" (1865) is unified by its intermittent reprise of lilac and star and bird.

In considering what sort of thinking a poet undertakes in composing a poem, one ought to mention as well the temptations that the poet's mind encounters along the way (for example, a temptation to sentimentality), and how these are staved off or (in some cases) yielded to. After taking up the three poems named above as examples of reprise, I want to come back to this question, and ask about the temptations Whitman faced as he wrote the poems.

"Sparkles from the Wheel" (1871) is an impeccable example of the reprise-poem, and will reveal what I mean by the poetic thinking that turns perceptions into perceptions-as-thoughts. The mode of thinking here I will call by Whitman's own term, *effusing*. It consists of a conscious refusal to remain a withdrawn spectator, and it requires, for its operation, an annihilation of personal identity. Whitman suggests how this form of empathetic thinking affects our sense of the world by showing us, in "Sparkles from the Wheel," the difference between describing the world when one is emotionally distant from it and describing it when one has "effused" oneself into it and devised new language for it from that fusion. Far from being the monster of egotism he has sometimes been thought to be, Whitman was a master of self-effacement, never more clearly than in his moments of "effusing."

"Sparkles from the Wheel" is divided into two sections; in each, the poet describes exactly the same scene, in which a knife-grinder, watched by a group of children, makes sparks fly as he sharpens a knife by turning his grinding stone. Here is the first scene: it is narrated by Whitman-the-withdrawn-spectator, and it is phrased in an active present tense indicative: "I pause; a knife-grinder works; sparkles from the wheel issue forth":

Sparkles from the Wheel

Where the city's ceaseless crowd moves on the livelong day,
Withdrawn I join a group of children watching, I pause aside with them.

By the curb toward the edge of the flagging,
A knife-grinder works at his wheel sharpening a great knife,
Bending over he carefully holds it to the stone, by foot and knee,
With measur'd tread he turns rapidly, as he presses with light but firm hand,

Forth issue then in copious golden jets,
Sparkles from the wheel.

Most readers would identify this as a poem by Whitman: it seems to contain his alert observation, his interest in the skilled workingman, his recognition of the unexpected beauty of everyday moments. But for Whitman himself this was not an acceptable poem. He could not end the composition here, because it would have remained solely transcriptive. This is indeed the writing of "retinal innocence," and if the poem stopped here, Santayana's description would be justified. But the intellect enters, and it is this that both motivates and characterizes the second half of the poem:

> The scene and all its belongings, how they seize and affect
>   me,
> The sad sharp-chinn'd old man with worn clothes and
>   broad shoulder-band of leather,
> Myself effusing and fluid, a phantom curiously floating,
>   now here absorb'd and arrested,
> The group, (an unminded point set in a vast surrounding,)
> The attentive, quiet children, the loud, proud, restive base
>   of the streets,
> The low hoarse purr of the whirling stone, the light-press'd
>   blade,
> Diffusing, dropping, sideways-darting, in tiny showers of
>   gold,
> Sparkles from the wheel.

Whitman repeats, in his second-stanza reprise, almost all the elements of the first scene. But this time those elements are named by a speaker who has placed himself in a markedly altered relation to the scene. Whitman makes the change explicit in the line that serves as a hinge between the original perceptual *gestalt* and its reprise as thought:

The scene and all its belongings, how they seize and affect
me.

The poet, now that he is seized and affected, adds human response
to perceptual registration. He begins to see the knife-grinder not as
a mechanical function but as an individualized man—sad, sharp-
chinned, old, ill-dressed, and bearing the badge of his profession in
the leather strap that he will loop to wheel and treadle:

The sad sharp-chinn'd old man with worn clothes and
broad shoulder-band of leather.

The order of Whitman's adjectives, at least in his more considered
poems such as this, is rarely arbitrary. Rather, the poetic mind is at
work applying its categories, of which the first is always "What
emotion governs the scene?" The poet is affected and seized first of
all by the feeling permanently etched on the face of the knife-
grinder, sadness; second, he is seized (as a painter might be) by the
man's defining visual outline, his sharp chin; third, by the knife-
grinder's age as an element of pathos; fourth, by his accoutre-
ments, of which the first, *worn clothes* (offered in lieu of an ad-
ditional visual effect such as *a blue shirt),* indicates his economic
status, while the second, the *shoulder-band of leather,* represents his
means of livelihood. Each of these perceptions-become-thoughts
has been evoked by the poet's almost unconscious scanning of
the knife-grinder, applying various categories already a part of his
rich taxonomic repertoire: *Predominant emotion? Physical identifying
marks? Age? Economic status? Line of work?* Although some of these
are merely sociological identifiers, the fact that Whitman places
emotion first, through the adjective *sad,* suggests that his catego-
ries of thought are not drawn from sociology alone. Nevertheless,
Whitman's internal checklist of thought-categories resembles, at
first glance, that of a sociologist putting his perceptions in order by
means of a standard internal table of classifiers.

One expects Whitman to go on characterizing, in this "seized" and "affected" manner, the other elements of the scene. And so he will. But before he can do so, he stops to add another element to his poetic thinking. Although the first act of thinking, for a poet, is to cultivate a receptivity to the world deeper than a merely visual one so that the scene may seize and affect him emotionally, and although the second act is to begin to make an intelligible classification of what he sees and senses, there is a third requisite for poetic thinking, given us in the next line. Here, Whitman is no longer a visual spectator, a receptive affected observer, or a sociologist, but rather a self-annihilator:

> Myself effusing and fluid, a phantom curiously floating,
>   now here absorb'd and arrested.

The words that Whitman is driven to in this account—his attempt in the second half of the poem to describe first the active, then the neutral, then the passive forms of his poetic thinking—are worth a look. *Effusing* is the first act: it can be defined as the act of "pouring out the spirit that was within," "melting one's inner self so as to enable it to pass outward"—this is an act of directed intellectual energy, will, and sympathy. The next psychological acts, the neutral ones, are odd, and are alliteratively linked: the poet becomes a *fluid phantom, floating.* "Effusing" himself, he dissolves his own solid outline, his own gravitational mass, his own identity, even his own material existence. In Whitman's quasi-scientific view of the cosmos, all the elements of the universe "float" eternally in a "solution" from which life precipitates out from time to time. The dead return to that solution. Here, by becoming a phantom, the poet is able to re-enter the solution and thereby to permeate the beings of others. The two passive adjectives, *absorb'd* and *arrested,* return us to *seized* and *affected,* asking us to compare the second passive formulation with the first one, to see how Whitman has revised his conceptualizing of the experience. To be *seized* is to retain one's own identity while being grasped by some other thing; but to be *absorbed* is to release one's identity as it is sucked into that of another (the Latin root is *ab-sorbere*, "to suck away"). To be *affected* is to find one's former identity modified; but to be *arrested* is to find one's former identity halted (the Latin root is *re-stare*, "to stand still") in favor of a self-annihilating effusion. Reflecting on his previous state, Whitman now realizes that he is lost and halted rather than grasped and modified; but by losing his personal identity, which he had deliberately guarded in his earlier "withdrawn" state, and by passing into the state of a floating phantom by being willing to liquefy and effuse himself, he can become the constituting poet of the scene rather than merely its distanced spectator, its intent receiver, or its interested sociologist. It is his "arrest" that gives him time and space to float, become a phantom, be absorbed, and, eventually, to write.

And we must notice one other departure from the sociologist of the first stanza: the sociologist would not have made the climax of his inventory the sparkles from the wheel of the grindstone. By ending on the visual rather than the sociological or even the psychological, Whitman sets the category "Beauty" as the final one to which his other classifiers tend, confirming his reprise-interest in the scene as crucially aesthetic (as well as convincingly sociological in its first, transcriptive, registering).

Here is the second registering of the scene, newly interpreted, in this reprise, by the poet who has now become—by all his curious active, neutral, and passive forms of thinking—part of it:

> The group, (an unminded point set in a vast surrounding,)
> The attentive, quiet children, the loud, proud, restive base
>   [for *bass*] of the streets,
> The low hoarse purr of the whirling stone, the light-press'd
>   blade,
> Diffusing, dropping, sideways-darting, in tiny showers of
>   gold,
> Sparkles from the wheel.

Although Whitman has already twice interrupted his second description for comment, those comments were about himself: they told us that he was affected, and that he responded by effusing himself and becoming a fluid floating phantom. But as soon as he resumes his scene, he is forced to interrupt himself yet again, this time to give us the fourth ingredient in that poetic thinking that acts upon the data of the innocent retina: besides willing an intent original attention, besides making order by classifying perceptions, besides exerting active sympathy even unto personal annihilation, the poet must adopt an aesthetic distance from his material. This is not the first-stanza distance of the withdrawn spectator, but the philosophical distance that arises when one adopts the viewpoint of indifferent Necessity. What is this little nineteenth-century American street-group to the impersonal universe? Nothing much, the thinking poet acknowledges: it is merely "an unminded point set in a vast surrounding." Whitman's stereoscopic thinking always considers human life as both acutely precious and completely insignificant. Affected as he is, absorbed as he is, "effused" as he is, the poet nonetheless can and must assume, if he is to rewrite perceptions into perceptions-as-thoughts, the detached perspective proper not only to philosophy but also to art.[6]

Only after Whitman has given us this fourth, detached, dimension of poetic thinking can he enact the full reprise of his original scene. How do the objects originally perceived change in the reprise when they become perceptions-infused-as-objectively-regarded-thoughts? The *children watching* are now felt in X-ray terms of their interior dispositions: they are *attentive and quiet*. The *city's ceaseless crowd,* formerly merely a numerical abstraction-in-motion, by becoming part of Whitman's being is granted emotions of its own: it is *loud, proud, restive.* The crowd has also been transmuted into music, assigned a part within the harmony of the scene, contributing the bass which accompanies the noise of the grindstone. The grindstone, no longer silent as it was in the first stanza, has acquired not only a musical tone of its own (both *low* and *hoarse*) but also an animal nature through its *purr.* In keeping with its animal voice, it now possesses independent motion: formerly it was turned by the knife-grinder, now it is *whirling* on its own, as Whitman enters into its being as well. The blade is the least transformed of the objects, but it is given nonetheless some animate existence, as Whitman feels himself into becoming the *light-press'd blade,* a blade that can feel the difference between being *light-pressed* and *heavy-pressed.* (In the first stanza, the blade, in all three of its appearances, was merely the object of the knife-grinder's action: *sharpening a great knife . . . he holds it . . . he presses with light but firm hand.*)

The sparkles from the wheel occur in the only line from the original scene which is preserved in identical form in the second part. This single instance of identical repetition calls our attention to the fact that the rest of the second scene is *not* mere repetition but a reprise, a re-invented description. It is the sparkles that undergo the most elaborate transmutation of all the elements of the scene. In their reappearance, their first verb—*diffusing*—matches the poet's *effusing:* because he has *effused,* the sparkles can, in an animate way, *diffuse* themselves. In the first stanza they only mechanically *issue,* but when their *issue* becomes *diffuse,* they gain an independent action of their own. Their diffusion is like the poet's own dissemination of himself into the elements of the scene. *Diffuse* is a word used of light; as the sparkles scatter from the wheel, they are first felt by the poet (as he kinesthetically becomes them) as pieces of light. The second verb used to describe the sparkles—*dropping*—makes them liquid, in synchrony with the poet's own newly-assumed fluid self. Their third verb—*sideways-darting*—gives the sparkles a volition comparable to that ascribed to the attentive children, the proud crowd, the purring stone, and the whirling wheel. And although in the non-poetic spectatorship of the first stanza, Whitman had seen the sparkles as copious *golden jets*—entities that could issue from a mechanism such as a fountain—he now, in mental identification with them, sees them as divine, in the form of those *showers of gold* in which Zeus has been known to manifest himself. The sparkles are, of course, divine emanations of a very miniature sort (this is, after all, only an inconspicuous street scene); and in resuming for a moment his long-distance cosmic view, Whitman says truly that they are only "tiny" showers of gold. But showers of gold, nonetheless, they are. We appreciate them further when we recall that Whitman said of the "American literat," "As he emits himself, facts are showered over with light."[7]

In short, the poet, by a voluntary mental yielding of his own identity into liquidity and even self-annihilation, must think his way into the independent and animate being of each thing he sees, from knife-grinder to grinding stone, conferring on each object, from the inner being he experiences as he inhabits it mentally, a language appropriate to its newly invested independence, emotions, volition, or music. As the poet decides to risk absconding from his own initial "withdrawnness," he is granted the sense of how it would feel to be a whirling stone or a darting sparkle, and the vision "from the inside" provides—as if "naturally"—the language that transforms an inventory into a poem.

I have reserved until now a mention of the most important difference between initial scene and reprise. Although the original scene is constructed, as I have said, as a chain of independent present-tense verbs *(I pause; the knife-grinder works; sparkles issue),* the reprise is constructed of noun-phrases, often accompanied by past or present participles *(Myself effusing; the group set; sparkles diffusing).* This grammatical feature tells us that poetic thinking must work to compress a multifaceted scene, distributed over sequential time, into a single momentary *gestalt;* and in this necessity we understand the concentration and focusing necessary to poetic thinking. We must imagine what it is to "instress" (to use the apposite word from Hopkins) in one's own being at one and the same moment all the motions of whirling and dropping and purring and being attentive and restive and lightly pressed, in order to get all one's words to combine into the correct multiphasic rendition of the *single* aura of the moment, not neglecting the knife-grinder's sadness that

shadows the otherwise joyous whole. I might add that Whitman is
not able, during his reprise, to gather the whole scene into a single
metaphor, but he does focus it down to two metaphorical figures:
the auditory harmony of voices and the visual radiation of light,
with the latter in the climactic position. It is poetic thinking—re-
quired to make poetry out of "retinal innocence"—that settles on
harmony and light as figures for its own activity.

When this little-remarked poem has been mentioned by critics
at all, it has been viewed as an *ars poetica* and summarized themati-
cally: the poet is the knife-grinder, and for the delight of the chil-
dren, he makes sparkling words.[8] Such readings do not take into ac-
count the fundamental genre of reprise which organizes the poem.
Looking at the function of reprise, we see that this poem enacts
the revision wrought by intense poetic thinking upon a perceptual
scene that streams in through sight and hearing. To change percep-
tion into a poem, the poet voluntarily registers and orders the
scene, and, by subjecting himself to it, allows it to absorb the self;
the scene is then philosophically distanced and linguistically formu-
lated. Reprise is the formal sign of distinct imaginative recasting,
by means of poetic thinking, of perceptions previously incoherent
or at least indifferent, because merely spectatorially and involun-
tarily received. The second-order formation of an aesthetic and lin-
guistic *gestalt* from a first-order perception is an act to which one
cannot refuse the name of thinking.

"Sparkles from the Wheel" is a scenic and descriptive poem.
How does Whitman think poetically when he is not primarily oc-
cupied with description? And what is the relation, in his poetics, of
description to incident? Whitman was so intensely a descriptive
poet, depending so fundamentally on sight and hearing (see, for ex-
ample, "Pictures" and "I Hear America Singing"), that narrative in-
cident—which continually attracts his historical attention—exists,
in his poetry, as an element in contention with lyric description.
Description and incident are always engaged in a competition—a
fact which usually enlivens the poetry. I want to take as an example
of this competition the Civil War lyric "Come Up from the Fields

Father." This poem has often been described as sentimental and melodramatic, and read thematically it might seem to exhibit both qualities. But it is not fair to Whitman—who put so much cunning into the construction of his poems—to read him solely thematically, because such readings ignore the mental energy expended in the writing of the poem and stored up in its lines. "Come Up from the Fields Father," like "Sparkles from the Wheel," has received almost no critical attention because it seems such a naive poem. Whitman, it has been suggested, may simply be transcribing in it an actual wartime incident.

Read for its story, "Come Up from the Fields Father" indeed appears artless. From the voice-over of a narrator, we learn that it is wartime, and that a rural Ohio family (consisting of a father, a mother, a son, and three daughters) has sent its son to the war. Life at the farm has gone on as before until the day a letter comes from the son, Pete ("his name is signed"). The eldest daughter, "just-grown"—who has presumably received the letter from the postman—calls to her father and mother to come to where she is, at the front door of the farmhouse. Although the letter transmits Pete's own "broken" sentences, it is not written in his hand. The narrator lets us know that even as the family absorbs the letter, the boy is already dead. The lyric ends with the mother's inconsolable grief.

Although the poem begins in the daughter's voice, she is soon interrupted by the voice of the narrator, and the poem becomes a formal reprise when the narrator, in lines 12 and 13, repeats the daughter's opening words—"Now from the fields come father . . . / And come to the entry mother"—but this time in his own voice, not hers:

Come Up from the Fields Father

Come up from the fields father, here's a letter from our
   Pete,
And come to the front door mother, here's a letter from
   thy dear son.

Lo, 'tis autumn,

Lo, where the trees, deeper green, yellower and redder,

Cool and sweeten Ohio's villages with leaves fluttering in
the moderate wind,

Where apples ripe in the orchards hang and grapes on the
trellis'd vines,

(Smell you the smell of the grapes on the vines?

Smell you the buckwheat where the bees were lately
buzzing?)

Above all, lo, the sky so calm, so transparent after the rain,
and with wondrous clouds,

Below, too, all calm, all vital and beautiful, and the farm
prospers well.

Down in the fields all prospers well,

But now from the fields come father, come at the
daughter's call,

And come to the entry mother, to the front door come
right away.

Fast as she can she hurries, something ominous, her steps
trembling,

She does not tarry to smooth her hair nor adjust her cap.

Open the envelope quickly,

O this is not our son's writing, yet his name is sign'd,

O a strange hand writes for our dear son, O stricken
mother's soul!

All swims before her eyes, flashes with black, she catches
the main words only,

Sentences broken, *gunshot wound in the breast, cavalry
skirmish, taken to hospital,*

At present low, but will soon be better.

Ah now the single figure to me,

Amid all teeming and wealthy Ohio with all its cities and
farms,

Sickly white in the face and dull in the head, very faint,
By the jamb of a door leans.
Grieve not so, dear mother, (the just-grown daughter speaks
through her sobs,
The little sisters huddle around speechless and dismay'd,)
See, dearest mother, the letter says Pete will soon be better.

Alas poor boy, he will never be better, (nor may-be needs
to be better, that brave and simple soul,)
While they stand at home at the door he is dead already,
The only son is dead.

But the mother needs to be better,
She with thin form presently drest in black,
By day her meals untouch'd, then at night fitfully sleeping,
often waking,
In the midnight waking, weeping, longing with one deep
longing,
O that she might withdraw unnoticed, silent from life
escape and withdraw,
To follow, to seek, to be with her dear dead son.
        [1865; 302–303]

What sort of poetic thinking do we see at work here? Before I con-
sider the poem as a reprise, I want to mention two of its other aes-
thetic strategies: the partition of space and the role of the narrator.
In terms of space, the poet sets the broadest of his concentric cir-
cles first, "Ohio's villages," but by the end space has narrowed to a
single point, the bereaved mother's bed. Whitman has decided to
divide the middle distance, the farm, into two regions: he does this
by organizing the poem spatially around the front door of the
farmhouse, which demarcates the father's territory—the fields—
from the mother's and daughters' territory—the house. The door
also demarcates public territory (the larger world from which the
letter arrives) from private territory (the domestic farm). Four
times the door punctuates the poem (lines 2, 13, 25, 30); everyone

gathers at the door, as poetic thinking geometrizes the events of the poem around that threshold.

We see poetic thought behind the construction of the narrator, too. He is made, first of all, to serve as the chorus representing onlooking America: his function is to say *Lo, Lo, lo, O, Ah, Alas,* and *O* (lines 3, 4, 9, 18, 22, 29, 36), surrounding the incident with the emotion of an unrelated voice, revealing the death of a soldier in wartime to be a collective rather than a private loss. Another of the narrator's functions is to be omniscient: it is he that tells us, from his godlike vantage-point, that Pete is already dead. Yet another of his functions is to serve as a directive lens, now in far-focus *(Lo, 'tis autumn . . . the trees / Cool and sweeten Ohio's villages),* now in close-focus *(Ah now the single figure to me . . . In the midnight waking, weeping).* These three functions—the choral, the omniscient, and the focus-setting—are the functions of spectatorial poetic thinking while it remains distant from its subject; consequently Whitman makes the narrator's lyric, but removed, voice alternate in antiphonal movement with the anguished "live" voices of the dramatis personae—daughter, mother, Pete.

The narrator, by his selectivity of detail, is the person who mediates the incident to us. He has the leisure for a heartfelt description of the farm in autumn, but none for the response of the father to his son's letter. By the omission of the father from all lines but the first, the narrator suggests that the father is not drawn into the circle of affection represented by the address of the distraught daughter to the mother *(dearest mother),* by the mother's reference to the son as *our dear son,* and by the narrator's reference to the affection between mother and son, *her* (not *their) dear dead son.* The mother, upon the death of her son, no longer wants to live: neither her husband nor her daughters can revive her from her grief. The narrator bequeaths this family to us, in their moment of tragedy, according to his own manner of selectivity and comment. (One can imagine a counter-poem, in which the narrator would tell the story from the father's point of view.)[9] Inevitably, when dealing with incident,

Whitman must decide from what "angle" he will tell the story. Deciding on plot-perspective (here, repressing the father's reaction) is also a function of poetic thinking, operating in its distance-mode.

Whitman's poetic thinking, then, has initially made the narrator omniscient and distanced. He can speak of events from the point of view of the cosmos (as did the speaker in the late moment of "Sparkles from the Wheel"), but he will drop that distance in the reprise, when he "effuses" himself into the domestic group and especially into the mother. Whitman's own aesthetic thinking is partitive, deciding the degree to which the poet will "infuse" himself into any scene or part of a scene. It is also reticent; it does not telegraph its own procedures. Much is left to the reader's capacity for inference. The poet does not mention the disastrous probable future of the family after the death of the son, but he expects us to realize it. (Pete is the only son, and the farm economy cannot continue long without him; there will be no one to replace the father in the fields as he ages; as the farm declines, the daughters will not have marriage-portions; the mother will remain withdrawn and depressed, leaving the "little sisters" with no mothering.) Whitman expects us to know all this consequence without his referring to it. (A sentimental poet would have spelled it out and drawn it out.)

Here, as in "Sparkles from the Wheel," the reprise makes distance give way to "effusion," and spectatorial observation to the self-annihilating moment of aesthetic fusion. Whitman's poetic thinking leads to the choice, for closure, of simultaneous present participles, representing, as in "Sparkles," the intense *gestalt* of aesthetic focus. He compresses the temporal incident at the farm into the successive verbals which make the mother's grief untensed and therefore eternal: *sleeping, waking, weeping, longing.* The contrary-to-fact subjunctive *(O that she might)* of the mother's dream extends itself in the subsequent untensed infinitives of impossibility: *to follow, to seek, to be with her dear dead son.* There is a missing, but longed-for, second door at the end of the poem: but the mother, dream as she may, cannot pass over its invisible threshold to join her son. As the narrator fuses with the mother, he annihilates himself. There is no narratorial conclusion from an omniscient distance to match the initial framing panorama of the Ohio villages.

I would not want to leave this example of poetic thinking without saying a word about the ornamental connections and repetitions among words in this poem. These are produced by the poet's phonetic compulsion to create the "binding secret" (Seamus Heaney's phrase) which makes the words of a poem seem purposefully magnetic toward each other, rather than accidentally related. The autumn landscape is introduced comparatively in order to show the natural and intensifying processes of organic life: the trees are "deeper green, yellower and redder." Their matching comparative is the wished-for (but not attained) vision of the son's life-progress which "ought" to parallel that of the trees: the letter says he "will soon be *better*." *Better*, says the boy's letter bravely; *better*, says the daughter hopefully; *better*, then says the narrator thrice, each time with a different emphasis and in a different tone:

(elegiacally) He will *never be* (physically) *better;*
(eulogistically) *nor may-be needs to be* (morally) *better;*
(diagnostically) *But the mother needs to be* (emotionally) *better.*

These five appearances of the word *better*—perspectivally prolonging the stoic *better* of the (phonetically matched) *letter* into the hopeful, the physical, the moral, and the emotional—show how poetic thinking can call attention to itself by reinscribing a word. As the poet repeats the word *better* (together with the four-times-repeated *door*, the thrice-repeated *letter*, and the narrator's multiple choral sighs), he creates the defining recurring supports of the reprise-poem.

If the family's actions and words stand for narrative incident, and the narrator for lyric description, we can see this poem as Whitman's reminder to himself that incident has its own rights: the family must be allowed their own "broken sentences" if they are to remain credible. *Come up from the fields father, here's a letter from our Pete . . . / O this is not our son's writing . . . the letter says Pete will soon be better.* This is the way the family talk, and their expression must be permitted to stand uncensored by "literary" intelligence. On the other hand, the language of the family is inadequate to delineate their suffering; the narrator therefore becomes their lyric supplement, "overlapping" with them in the poem's initiating of formal reprise, as the narrator repeats the daughter's initial cry, saying in his own rewriting, *But now from the fields come father, come at the daughter's call, / And come to the entry mother, to the front door come right away.* This reprise, as the narrator enters the scene that had previously belonged only to the family, is the sign of the narrator's passage from omniscience to empathy. If Whitman's intent in reprise is to annihilate himself in order to "become" and animate the elements of a scene (from unconscious children to sparkles from a wheel), what happens when the elements are already animate and adult, as here? What can the consciousness of the poet bring to the consciousness of other adult human beings? The poet refrains from "animating" the grieving mother into action; instead he gives his own language to her passionately animated grief, for which she herself has only tears, not words. As the "effusing" narrator and the grieving mother become a single sensibility in the fifth, sixth, and last stanzas, Whitman approaches a utopian solution to reprise in which the narrative objectivity of reported speech and third-person incident ("Come up from the fields father . . . she hurries") would fuse with lyric description ("Ah now the single figure to me") in a sympathetic alchemy, as narrative would become inseparable from its lyric reprise, in the process annihilating the omniscient and detached narrator.

In my third example, the famous little poem "A Noiseless Patient Spider," Whitman moves from narrative in the initial scene to allegory in the reprise, from description of the scene to direct address in the reprise. The poem is composed of two five-line stanzas, of which the first describes the spider and the second addresses the soul. As in "Sparkles from the Wheel" and "Come Up from the

Fields Father," the scene is written in tensed verbs, the reprise in a tenseless sequence of participles. I introduce this poem not to make the points I have already made—about the reprise as a signal that perception has been actively rethought as *gestalt,* or about the participle as a signal that an aesthetic moment, a tenseless poetic ingathering, has achieved closure—but rather to show poetic thinking apparently using reprise as an occasion for mere repetition, but in fact directing itself to imaginative reconception. The first stanza gives us the tireless seeking motions of the spider:

> A noiseless patient spider,
> I mark'd where on a little promontory it stood isolated,
> Mark'd how to explore the vacant vast surrounding,
> It launch'd forth filament, filament, filament, out of itself,
> Ever unreeling them, ever tirelessly speeding them.

We might pause here to notice that all the words that are repeated within this first element of the poem, the scene, recur in identical form: *mark'd* (to convey the invariant attention of the observer); *filament* (which suggests instinct's invariant production of the same thread each time); *ever* (together with the subsequent *tirelessly* the sign of invariant patience); and *them* (reiterating the production of invariant filaments). Against this background of unaltering repetitiveness, the variant verbs predicated of the spider become foregrounded. First the spider *stood;* then (in order to *explore*) it successively *launch'd forth* filaments, *unreeling* and *speeding* them. These are all actions predicable of human beings (as *extrudes,* for instance, could not be); and all of them, except for *stood,* have vaguely synonymous connotations. The speaker thinks first of the spider as an explorer, then as someone launching something (as one might launch a spear), then as someone unreeling something (as one might unreel a fishing-line), then as someone speeding something on its way (a transitive form of the verb *to speed* that can be used morally—to *bid Godspeed to*—as well as physically). If we inquire

into why (given these verbs) Whitman is speculating on the pro-
duction of filaments, we see that the spider's *launching* resembles
the poet's own *effusing* of himself, the *unreeling* suggests the inex-
haustible supply of the inner fiber of human connection, and the
speeding suggests the yearning hope that has motivated the launch-
ing in the first place.

It is only in the reprise, when the soul becomes Whitman's ex-
plicit and formal subject, that the remarks made with respect to the
spider intensify into true imaginative form. At first, the soul-reprise
seems, disappointingly, merely to restate the spider-case. The first
words used of the soul make us think we are encountering a *da
capo* repetition rather than a reprise, because they are identical to,
or very closely synonymous with, those used of the spider. The spi-
der *stood*, the soul *stands;* the *surrounding* around the spider is al-
most identically reiterated as we see the soul *surrounded;* where the
spider had been *isolated*, the soul is (not dissimilarly) *detached;* the
soul's position in *measureless oceans of space* is almost indistinguish-
able from that of the spider in its *vacant vast surrounding;* and if the
spider works *tirelessly*, the soul works (in an echo) *ceaselessly*. In
short, there seems to be little active poetic thinking: the poem ap-
pears to be not a true reprise but rather a palimpsest in which the
overlay is nearly the same as the underscript.

But the intellectual difference characteristic of true reprise be-
comes obvious once we move beyond the word *ceaselessly*. Now
we see that whatever the soul may be launching, it has no single
name such as "filament" at all. By contrast to the three utterings of
filament, the object launched by the soul remains conspicuously
unspecified. Rather, the soul is seen to have a potentially infinite
variety of activities, and many spheres of operation:

> And you O my soul where you stand,
> Surrounded, detached, in measureless oceans of space,
> Ceaselessly musing, venturing, throwing, seeking the
>   spheres to connect them,

Till the bridge you will need be form'd, till the ductile
    anchor hold,
Till the gossamer thread you fling catch somewhere, O my
    soul.
    [1868; *LG*, 450]

The five verbals defining the soul's actions—*musing, venturing,
throwing, seeking to connect,* and *fling*—lead us to ask what categories
they are representing for Whitman in his reprise, as he conjures up
the motions of his soul produced by his having effused himself
into the spider. The first, *musing,* is both an intellectual and an aes-
thetic word; we may all muse, mentally, but the poet's soul muses
assisted by the Muse. (This word comes from sensing anterior
intentionality in the spider's aim.) The second verbal, *venturing,* has
to do with Faith, since it presumes a result that is still unknown
(as in Columbus's venturing, the soul explores oceans unknown).
The third verbal, *throwing,* suggests that the soul has, so to speak,
sighted land—has reached a place in its venturing close enough to
its object to begin guiding the direction of its invisible "filaments."
When we come to *seeking to connect,* the fourth verbal, we see that
it has to do with Hope rather than Faith, since it now has an envis-
aged object—a sphere or spheres—that can be connected to each
other or to itself if only they can be found.[10] The spider was an ex-
plorer and a launcher too, but, because it operates on instinct, it
cannot be said to be in the intentional sense a seeker, nor to possess
an infinitive of intent, such as *to connect.* I defer mention of the fifth
verbal, *fling,* to its proper place at the close.

The closing two lines of the second stanza are not, formally, part
of the reprise, since in them we enter the moment when both
Faith (the evidence of things unseen) and Hope (represented in
Christian iconography by an anchor) now desire their fulfillment in
Love. Just as the soul has been given five activities, its spiritual "fila-
ment" is now given three names: it is a *bridge,* an *anchor,* and a *gos-
samer thread.* It is clear that the last of these brings us closest to the

spider. The first of the nouns, the *bridge,* is created by the poet to bear the speaker's human weight as his soul crosses over to the sphere of the beloved; the second, the *anchor,* is created to arrest his former restless venturing; and the third, the *gossamer thread,* as it reconnects us to the spider, suggests the fragility of desire.

I return now to the last verb invented for the soul, as the narrator says that it *flings* its thread. *To fling* is differentiated from *to throw* by its connotations of impulse and abandon: in this last verb Whitman acknowledges the risk of abandoning oneself to the recklessness of Hope and Faith—and, above all, to Love. The images attached to Faith *(bridge . . . be form'd)* and to Hope *(anchor hold)* lack a *terminus ad quem;* and while the transitive verb first associated with Love *(fling)* has an object (the *gossamer thread),* that filament proceeds to an intransitive verb of its own *(catch),* which can attain in imagination no direct object such as the *sphere* earlier envisaged. The uncertainty of *till,* no matter how confidently it is initially voiced, is borne out by the fact that the hoped-for beloved can be located only in an intransitive verb *(catch)* and an indefinite adverb *(somewhere).* The undermining that results from the intransitive verb and its indefinite adverb shades the tone of hope with elegy, as the poem ends. As we look back at the poem we see, first, the spider engaged in invariant, because instinctual, actions; then an allegorical reprise of the spider's actions transferred, with a signal deepening of reference in the multiplying of verbs, to the intentional realm of human Faith and Hope; and then the coda in which, departing from reprise, the poet allows himself to imagine the unseen and almost despaired-of end, when the soul that believes all things and hopes all things may eventually find its object of love.

We can see Whitman's process of thinking as he discovers in succession, for his scene and its reprise, the "identical" words he needs and their order; the non-identical verbs and nouns he needs and *their* order; the extent of overlap he can believably construct between the spider and his soul; and the departure from reprise in the future-directed coda by which the emotional bridge-making and anchoring of love go beyond anything we can imagine in the instinctually-controlled spider. We can also see Whitman's process of thinking as a form of transmutation, since he takes up the Christian virtues of Faith, Hope, and Love, and, first naturalizing them by means of the spider, subsequently returns them to the realm of value as he resituates them in the soul, relocating their object from the Pauline divine realm to the human erotic domain. The noiselessness initially predicated (incomprehensibly) of the spider, we now understand, is a back-formation from the reprise; the spider must be "noiseless" because all the activity of the questing soul takes place in the silent domain of unspoken yearning, since the words of love cannot be articulated until their object is found.

Each of these three poems of reprise—"Sparkles from the Wheel," "Come Up from the Fields Father," and "A Noiseless Patient Spider"—begins in a life-incident: a street scene of knife-sharpening; the anguish of a rural family whose son has been wounded in the war; a spider's efforts to begin a web. In all three, I think, the poet visibly resists the temptations of insufficiently examined response. In composing "Sparkles from the Wheel," for instance, Whitman suffers three temptations. Tempted by sociology, he at first indulges the temptation to do a spectatorial genre-painting; but then he departs from that picture into a form of mental activity by which he imagines what it would be like to be not only a knife-grinder but a grindstone, a crowd, a knife, and a shower of sparkles. While in this state—his "effused" phantom-annihilation—he finds the original and appropriate language for each of his newly assumed existences. Tempted by human intimacy to a naive participation in the scene analogous to that of the bystander-children, the poet both indulges that thoughtless union and then moves far away from it to note the lack of cosmic importance of the very scene he celebrates. Tempted by his artisanal admiration for labor and a political wish for democratic solidarity, the poet in-

dulges those temptations and yet finally endorses, in the climax of
the poem, something else as well—the "useless" and non-human,
but beautiful, showers of gold from the wheel. In the case of each
temptation, the poet has examined his first, superficial, response
and complicated it by a counter-pull which he finds in his own
moral and poetic intelligence.

The temptations undergone by Whitman as he writes "Come
Up from the Fields Father" are somewhat different. He is tempted
to let the poem become simply its own narrative, as it would if it
were a ballad (Whitman had written sentimental ballads on com-
parable topics in his youth).[11] The poet indulges this temptation
by including the "unedited" utterances of the family, but counters
it by not letting them dictate entirely the tone and language of
the poem. Something, after all, must still belong to the sphere of
the poet, whose powers of expression and arrangement are more
greatly developed than those of the suffering family.

In "Come Up from the Fields Father" Whitman is also tempted
by dramatic irony, and indulges it as the narrator intones "The
farm prospers well" while, unbeknownst to the family, the son has
already died. But Whitman never returns to this tone of irony in
the rest of the poem: he refuses to be permanently superior to the
events he recites. The poet is also tempted by the cosmic view, one
that can see at once all of "Ohio's villages," a panorama of which
this farm, after all, is only a small part. After indulging this tempta-
tion with the poem's superb view of the autumn, with its multiple
rejoicings of the senses (in the words *sweeten, fluttering, smell, buzz-
ing*), Whitman rejects the large overview, or even the middle view
of the entire family, in favor of effusing himself into the afflicted
"single figure" at the close, the mother who is emotionally more
consequential to him than all the sensual fulfillments of autumn.
Yet he achieves at the end a philosophical detachment from the
mother's desire, by referring to her son not (as she would) as *her
dear son* but as *her dear dead son.*

"Come Up from the Fields Father" is also tempted, I think, by the form of reprise itself. After the daughter's call opens the poem, the narrator reopens the poem with the same call in his own voice, echoing hers, as if he aimed to appropriate entirely within his own utterance the voice of the grieving family.[12] But he resists this temptation to incorporate, into a normative lyric spoken by his single voice, the words of the characters of his poem; instead he creates—following the narrator's moment of exact reprise—a quasi-dramatic lyric, in which the characters of the poem are allowed their language side-by-side with the poet's own. We see the ghost of reprise in the repeated, but always resituated, three words *door, letter, better* (to which we could add the mother's black grief [*black,* lines 19, 33; *in the midnight,* line 35]). These repetitions give credence to a desire, on the poet's part, for that regular symmetry that we associate with the static structure of mirroring reprise. Yet Whitman finally rejects, after summoning it, the iterative stasis of binary reprise in favor of the tragic onward deepening of the mother's grief (which gives the poem its ultimately linear structure): *she hurries, she does not tarry, all swims before her eyes, sickly white in the face, drest in black, waking, weeping, with her dear dead son.* In the temptation to write a reprise that significantly alters the initial tableau by his own "effusion," a temptation indulged by echo and then rejected as the narrator is absorbed within the mother, we see the poet interrogating his own compositional impulses as the poem progresses.

Does "A Noiseless Patient Spider," too, show evidence of temptations indulged and rejected? Or of temptations indulged and not rejected? It is more allegorical and self-explanatory, perhaps, than Whitman's greatest work (and consequently has been a favorite in textbooks for younger students). Perhaps the neatness of its allegorizing represents an Emersonian temptation *not* rejected. Whitman must have been tempted (if only by a spider's foreseeable success in attaching its filament) to imagine a happy ending for the soul's quest, some paradise of erotic satisfaction. But this choice, even if voiced in the future of "until," would have made the poem too optimistic in view of the vicissitudes of human desire. If we imagine an ending such as "Till the gossamer thread you fling be caught to the breast of a friend," we can better appreciate Whitman's final tragic catch at *somewhere*. He resists—through the mind's sad skepticism and its sense of aesthetic propriety—the temptation to give fulfillment a material "sphere."

Whitman is too copious and inventive and fierce an author to be easily described, and his inquiries into possible poetic means, his exhaustive linguistic investigations, and his discrimination in both approved and rejected choices need to be seen afresh in each poem.[13] He is too subtle to be comprehended by such wide-grained leading ideas as nationalism, democracy, the body, and gender. He is too intellectual to be seen solely as a poet of enthusiastic sociological transcription of American scene and event, too mournful to be summed up as a celebrant of nineteenth-century expansion, too idiosyncratic to be subsumed into the history of American oratory. When Emerson, in 1855, justly called *Leaves of Grass* "the most extraordinary piece of wit and wisdom that America has yet contributed," he was praising, by the words "wit" and "wisdom," Whitman's intellectual perspicacity. When he continued, "I give you joy of your free and brave thought," he was greeting Whitman as an original thinker and an equal in courageous conceptualization. When he said he found in the poems "incomparable things said incomparably well," he suggested, by the identity of his adjective and adverb, Whitman's matching of considered stylistic means to distinctive intellectual content—the quality I have been emphasizing here. Almost a century ago, Ezra Pound wrote of Whitman, "I think we have not yet paid enough attention to the deliberate artistry of the man, not in details but in the large."[14] The artistry of both the large and the details still remains, in great part, to be discovered. When we understand Whitman's poetics more deeply, especially in his re-invention and elaboration of familiar lyric genres, we will be able to give a more persuasive view of the sort of imaginative thinking that underlies the ever-surprising surfaces of Whitman's work.

→ 3 ←

Emily Dickinson Thinking

REARRANGING SERIALITY

The Inner – paints the Outer –
The Brush without the Hand –
Its Picture publishes – precise –
As is the inner Brand.[1]

IT IS NATURAL that Emily Dickinson's work should come to mind
when one reflects on the evidence for thinking in poetry. Her po-
ems have been called metaphysical, philosophical, theological. Vo-
cabularies have been invented to describe her style of thinking—its
cryptic ellipses, its compression, its enigmatic subjects, its absent
centers, and its abstraction. These qualities indeed are her "carbon-
ates"—the residue of the fire that preceded them: "Ashes denote
that Fire was" [1097; 1865]. But there is another quality that is
equally intrinsic to her verse, and that is Dickinson's invention of
poetic temporal structures that mimic the structure of life as she at
any moment conceives it. By those structures she channels our re-
actions, stylizes our pace to hers, and constructs our thinking after
her own. Any detailed assertions about her work must be partial
ones in view of the almost 1800 poems she composed. Nonethe-
less, I think there is something to be said about her thinking as she
invents ways to plot temporality.[2]

The larger ideas in Dickinson are not recondite ones: she sati-
rizes received religious thought while retaining its metaphysical di-
mension and much of its compensatory solace; she continues the
European lyric description of how erotic adoration comes to grief;

64

and she dwells a great deal on nature's appearances, death's certainty, and an uncertain immortality. If Dickinson's themes are not the determinant of her style of thinking, what is? Her well-described grammatical and syntactic and metaphorical idiosyncrasies certainly play a central role in conveying her style of thought to us, but to understand her imaginative thinking we also need to perceive how, in her poems, she alters "normal" temporal organization. I take for granted the usual critical account, derived from the poetry, of Dickinson's emotional crises, in which a soul of intense sensitivity, hoping to find stability in religion or love, is brought to grief by some unidentified rupture. The grief, which leads almost to madness, is sometimes represented as a psychological death. After each such crisis, the poet experiences a long aftermath[3] marked by new traumas reinscribed on the old, intermitted by forms of denial, stoicism, and regressive idealization. I will be paying particular attention to how Dickinson orders the inner structure of her poems to represent the way such life-events reshape one's conception of serial existence itself.

I believe that Dickinson's early and "natural" style of thinking about serial plot aimed at a temporal exhaustiveness: her youthful poems unscrolled, like her sun, "a ribbon at a time," and wished to project, by displaying one "ribbon" after another, a complete coverage of temporal experience from beginning to a definite end. These early poems tended to believe not only that all roads have an end, but also that "all roads" have "A 'Clearing' at the end," as she says in the 1859 poem "My Wheel is in the dark" [61]. En route to the dénouement at the clearing, the early poems aimed to string out experience phase by phase, aspiring to leave no gaps in event or perception before arriving at the end of the sequence. The 1861 poem "I'll tell you how the Sun rose –" [204] generated four such "ribbons," each characteristically possessing a distinctively active verb:

> The Steeples swam in Amethyst!
> The news like squirrels ran!

The hills untied their Bonnets!
The Bobolinks begun!

Dickinson paid out her successive ribbons of active verbs again in
her 1862 poem on the locomotive: "I like to see it lap the Miles – /
And lick the Valleys up" [383].[4] Because the train is said to com-
plain "In horrid – hooting stanza," we can see this early exercise as
in part a self-reflective *ars poetica:* "I like to see it do X and Y . . .
And then . . . And then . . . Then . . . And . . . Then." The poet's ac-
tive work of thinking "fills up" with serial incidents the extended
journey of the train, just as her thinking had "filled up" the rising
of the sun with serial "ribbons." In each case, the impression is
given that all of the manifest phenomena have been noted, since
the rising of the sun is followed in the poem by its setting, and the
beginning of the train's journey is completed when it stops "At its
own stable door."

I adopt the term "chromatic" from musicology to express Dick-
inson's need in such poems to sound, in exhaustive sequence, every
note in a scale—black and white, step and half-step. Her compul-
sion to a "chromatic" form of thinking is what Dickinson her-
self called, in an early poem, "Notching the fall of the even sun"
["Bound – a trouble –"; 240; 1861].[5] Although the poet is in fact
making up the "slots" she is *filling* up, the early poems wished to ob-
scure that constructive invention, and to appear merely transcrip-
tive. If the train stops at tanks, goes around mountains, peers in
shanties, crawls between the cliffs of a quarry, and chases itself
downhill, we are meant to believe that the narrator saw the shan-
ties and the quarry, the mountains and the tanks. If, by contrast, we
felt the poem were being "made up," we would feel anxiety that
the train-journey might be prolonged forever in other landscapes,
new stops. The anxiety attendant on Zeno's paradox—the fact that
time is infinitely divisible—lies behind Dickinson's attempt to mas-
ter that paradox by pretending that the train has only a limited
number of places to pass before it stops, that the sun has only a

certain number of phenomena to exhibit before it has exhausted its
"ribbons" of rising. Once you have pointed out the effect of the
dawn on the steeples, the squirrels, the hills, and the bobolinks,
you have finished, and your anxiety is appeased.

Dickinson's inch-by-inch chromatic scale bares the hidden anxi-
ety behind its construction when the leisurely, pleasant, and widely
separated *and then*'s of the jaunty train turn into the immediately
successive, grim, and inflexible *and then*'s of a torturer's chamber.
We find, in "The Heart asks Pleasure – first –" of 1863, the "same"
kind of poem, the "same" form of "notched" chromatic thinking,
the "same" structure of inch-by-inch unrolling of ribbon and filling
of slots. Now, however, the seriality that had earlier seemed so un-
troubled and solacing extends itself to the horror of time's infinite
divisibility, matched by the terror of a loss of personal control over
the termination of sequence. This road has no clearing at the end:

> The Heart asks Pleasure – first –
> And then – excuse from Pain –
> And then – those little Anodynes
> That deaden suffering –
>
> And then – to go to sleep –
> And then – if it should be
> The will of its Inquisitor
> The privilege to die –
> [588; 1863]

This little poem imitates, in its seriality, the ratcheting of the wheel
on which the victim is stretched. Once the single clause *The Heart
asks* generates the rest of the poem, we find no bustling quanta of
active verbs (as in the poems of sunrise and train-journey) propel-
ling the *and then*'s. In the first stanza, the objects of the Heart's ask-
ing are nouns—*Pleasure, excuse, Anodynes*—boons that might be ob-
tained from a benevolent superior. In the second stanza, the objects

of the Heart's asking are inactive verbs of state: *to go to sleep; to die.*
As the positive goods requested in the first stanza, and even the
forms of unconsciousness implored in the second, are refused, the
poem spreads its syntax out, abandoning its peremptory terseness
for a pitiful groveling. How boldly the Heart had asked "Pleasure –
first –"; how reduced it has become, as it begs that there be a last
stage to this process.[6] Thought is unable to control the chromatic
scale here in the way it could when Dickinson could expect the rib-
boned sun to set predictably or could bring the train to a stable
stop at its stable door; instead, Fate alone holds the power to deter-
mine the unknown end of torture. The poet now sees that her abil-
ity to think up a plot is in contention with Fate's own plotting; and
peaceful slot-filling seriality is the casualty of this recognition.

In other Dickinson poems we find that thought has lost not only
existential mastery of sequence but also cognitive dominion over
sense perception. Perceptions simply crowd in too thick and fast to
be arrangeable in a single chromatic sequence. In an 1863 poem on
the sunset, Dickinson shows herself, in the face of nature's multi-
plicity of effects, unable to produce a regular exhaustive progres-
sion of the sort we have seen in sunrise, train, and torture. Now so
many categories for inclusion in the sequence present themselves
at once that the emotional result of such profusion is not, Dickin-
son says, sequential comprehensiveness, but ignorance:

> An ignorance a Sunset
> Confer upon the Eye –
> Of Territory – Color –
> Circumference – Decay –
>
> Its Amber Revelation
> Exhilarate – Debase –
> Omnipotence' inspection
> Of Our inferior face –
>
> And when the solemn features
> Confirm – in Victory –

We start – as if detected
In Immortality.
[669; 1863]

The definite opening and closure here resemble those of the po-
ems cited earlier: we begin at the beginning of the sunset, and we
end with the Victory and Immortality associated by religion with
the end of life. But the would-be chromatic middle part is troubled
as it was not in the past; too many categories apply for individual
exhaustiveness of treatment. Territory? Color? Circumference? De-
cay? Where to begin? Each material category named by Dickinson
implies that there should be within it a step-by-step temporal un-
folding: the spread of the sunset over the *territory* varies; the *colors*
change as the sunset progresses; the sunset's *circumference* in the
heavens mutates; its beauty will gradually *decay*. Dickinson demon-
strates that the emotional "slots" to be filled here exhibit the same
confusing multiplicity as the material ones of the second stanza:
should one express one's *exhilaration* at the spectacle or one's feel-
ing of being *debased* in comparison to its glory? The poet's asserted
incompetence to match the revelation with words generates in her
the postlapsarian shame felt in anticipating God's *inspection*, from
which one hides one's *inferior* face as did Adam and Eve in the gar-
den. Although the religious close of this sunset poem attempts—
through the word "confirm"—resolution in the earlier vein of "set-
ting" or "stopping," the failure to exhaust the many potential chro-
matic scales of the poem is made to generate a frustrated, even a
guilty, response, one that is scattered and confused both descrip-
tively and emotionally. The sensuous world of "Omnipotence" is
less predictable, even, than the ("as if detected") prison-world of an
earthly Inquisitor, and the tremor of ignorance, with its "as if," is
shown—in Dickinsonian skepticism—to shake the confidence of
the closure in Immortality.

In sacrificing the neatness of the serial *and then*, in multiplying
her material and emotional slots beyond the possibility of filling
them, in making ignorance the revelation of the sunset, Dickinson

shows that, far from forsaking her chromaticism—her wish for an exhaustive description of experience—she is letting it lead her in unforeseen directions. A seriality without gaps remains forever, I believe, the first resort of her mind when she begins to think. Even when—as in "He scanned it – Staggered –"—she allows the attempt at full serial comprehension to lead first to blindness and then to suicide, she stays determinedly on the rails of a chromatic serial inquiry, seamlessly connecting a beginning to a middle and an end. Here, however, the active verbs become chiefly not material but epistemological *(scan, caught at a sense, groped)*:

> He scanned it – Staggered –
> Dropped the Loop
> To Past or Period –
> Caught helpless at a sense as if
> His Mind were going blind –
>
> Groped up, to see if God were there –
> Groped backward at Himself
> Caressed a Trigger absently
> And wandered out of Life –
>   [994; 1865]

To the man in despair, the gaping slots on the way to certitude are wholly unfillable in any satisfying way: scan as he will, catch at sense though he may, grope to God though he try, grope to self though he retreat, he can make no sense of the world before him, past or present. Without time, which he has "dropped," there can be no intelligible construction of sequence. His last friend is the trigger that frees him from his unintelligible serial existence and lets him, at last, emotionally "wander" to no destination.

It is clear from "He scanned it –" that this method of thinking—in which it is hoped that systematic inquiry, asking or groping in chromatic sequence, will eventually "solve" the emotional crisis and bring closure—has become bankrupt for Dickinson.[7] She has come to feel (as she later puts it) that "Capacity to terminate / Is a specific Grace –" [1238; 1871], and when it is denied her, she will, metaphorically speaking, caress a trigger—that is, represent herself as already dead, or quasi-dead.

The great crisis in Dickinson's work arrives when her instinctive practice of serial "filled-up" chromatic advance encounters unavoidable fissure, fracture, rupture, or abyss. This is the crisis that any writer wedded to serial chromaticism would be bound to face. Over the years, Dickinson writes many poems recounting rupture of all serene or predictable forms of serial plot. The poem in which the concept of "Sequence" is explicitly mentioned is the 1864 poem called "I felt a Cleaving in my Mind –." The mind, Dickinson acknowledges, no longer obeys the will that wishes to assemble thoughts in a seamless continuum (as notes are assembled in music):

> The thought behind, I strove to join
> Unto the thought before –
> But Sequence ravelled out of Sound –
> Like Balls – upon a Floor –[8]
> [867; 1864]

As sound ceases to display a meaningful sequence of tones, so thought unspools itself out of reach.

Poems written earlier than "I felt a Cleaving in my Mind –" cannot quite consent to the unraveling of sequence. The best-known of these earlier poems about rupture is the 1862 "I felt a Funeral, in my Brain," written in a posthumous voice. It seems to have found a terminus to its sequence, in that it retells the break as the process, from beginning to end, of the speaker's funeral (which one takes at first as a metaphor for final closure); and it is psychologically still wedded (as "I felt a Cleaving in my Mind –" is not) to the structural form of exhaustive sequence and dénouement. Yet this poem be-

trays its new bewilderment concerning the representation of the
end of serial experience by constructing alternate conclusions to its
narrative, neither of which is the expected burial underground that
"ought" to follow a funeral. In the first ending, in stanza four, the
speaker is imagined as leading a solitary "wrecked" life, coffined
but conscious:

> I felt a Funeral, in my Brain,
> And Mourners to and fro
> Kept treading – treading – till it seemed
> That Sense was breaking through –
>
> And when they all were seated,
> A Service, like a Drum –
> Kept beating – beating – till I thought
> My mind was going numb –
>
> And then I heard them lift a Box
> And creak across my Soul
> With those same Boots of Lead, again,
> Then Space – began to toll,
>
> As all the Heavens were a Bell,
> And Being, but an Ear,
> And I, and Silence, some strange Race
> Wrecked, solitary, here –

However, Dickinson unexpectedly adds a second ending. Although
the poem "should" have ended here, at the penultimate stanza,
Dickinson reveals that her mind cannot maintain the stasis and sta-
bility of that sepulchral survival. Her floor of Reason suddenly
gives way, and she falls further and further into the abyss, at each
stage colliding with a plane of existence, until consciousness is
wholly abolished:

And then a Plank in Reason, broke,
And I dropped down, and down –
And hit a World, at every plunge,
And Finished knowing – then –
                    [340; 1862][9]

Ritual (Dickinson's most solemn form of processional exhaus-
tive chromatic order) is enacted here in the familiar successive
phases of the funeral and its aftermath: the entrance of the
mourners, the church service, the exit of the mourners with the
coffin, and the tolling of the funeral knell. Yet the serial progress
suggested by these sequential phases is countered by the stasis im-
plied by the repetitions within the phases: "treading – treading /
beating – beating –/ . . . those same Boots of Lead, again, / . . .
Space – began to toll, / I dropped down, and down –/ And hit a
World, at every plunge." These tormenting repetitions of obsessive
thinking, persisting through the break in Reason, are formally abol-
ished only by the unconsciousness that follows the traumatic falls.
The speaker's collapse reveals that although ritual and other such
exhaustive chromatic orderings have in the past kept existence in-
telligible for her, this rupture, persistently reasserting itself by repe-
tition of static moves, is stronger than reassuring ritual. Desolation
is figured as the absence of sequential motion in an apparently
final, wrecked, "here," but obsession cannot be arrested: instead,
Madness brings great unforeseen plunges which are the opposite
of ritually controlled chromatic motion toward a rationally antici-
pated end. The last destination is not a knowable place but a post-
humously-pronounced time—a "then" unavailable to conscious-
ness.

   The unconsciousness to which Dickinson resorts to bring "I felt
a Funeral" to some kind of *terminus ad quem* cannot be a satisfac-
tory end for an inquisitive mind, which must return, even after cri-
sis, to some sort of apprehension: "No Drug for Consciousness –

can be –" ["Severer Service of myself"; 887; 1864]. But since noth-
ing further can possibly happen in life—or so the wounded soul
feels—something has to happen to sequence itself, something that
can replace its normal *and then*'s which lead to an end. In the 1862
poem "After great pain, a formal feeling comes –" Dickinson imag-
ines a structure which is still one of sequence; but this sequence,
though serial, is not linear: the speaker's feet enact a circular repeti-
tive sequence made meaningless by emotional apathy. Because of
her indifference, her emotional deadness, the speaker links her ac-
tions not by progressive *and then*'s but by meaningless *or*'s:

> After great pain, a formal feeling comes –
> The Nerves sit ceremonious, like Tombs –
> The stiff Heart questions 'was it He, that bore,'
> And 'Yesterday, or Centuries before'?
>
> The Feet, mechanical, go round –
> A Wooden way
> Of Ground, or Air, or Ought –
> Regardless grown,
> A Quartz contentment, like a stone.
>
> This is the Hour of Lead –
> Remembered, if outlived,
> As Freezing persons, recollect the Snow –
> First – Chill – then Stupor – then the letting go.
>   [372; 1862]

The speaker of "After great pain" is not, in fact, dead; it is only
"the glittering retinue of Nerves" ["Severer Service of myself";
887; 1864] that have become "like Tombs –." In aftermath, the
speaker feels uncertainty not only about identity ("was it He [*or* I]
that bore") but also about time (did it happen "Yesterday, or Cen-
turies before?"). A formal and monumental "posthumous" present
tense of state reigns in lieu of sequence: "The Nerves *sit ceremoni-*

ous, like Tombs." Chromatic linear advance has vanished in favor of repetitive circling, a new form of unavailing ritual: "The Feet, mechanical, go *round.*" Some parts of the body have already undergone rigor mortis: flesh has become *wooden,* and the formerly pulsing heart is *stiff.* The feet are indifferent ("regardless") concerning the character of the floor they mechanically tread: the floor could equally well be named terrestrial "Ground" *or* ethereal "Air" *or* moral "Ought." The emotions experience "A Quartz contentment, like a stone."[10] Quartz, a vitreous crystal, is the birthstone, so to speak, of this poem—once a glassy fluid, it too has suffered rigor mortis. Insofar as the "formal feeling" can be described, it is like a stone in its immobility; but it is not amorphous: it is tensely rigid with its own self-interlocking crystal-lattice that cannot be rearranged.

The metrical irregularity of the second stanza of "After great pain" marks, I believe, Dickinson's sensing of the difference between chromatic *advance* (marked by the *and then* of true sequence) and the faux-chromatic *repetition* of aftermath. In the latter state one still moves step by step, with every second of existence exhaustively marked, but one can move only in an incrementally traced circle—a prisoner's circuit within confined bounds, one that remains on a level plane and leads nowhere. In the final simile of "After great pain," Dickinson relents into sequence *(then . . . then);* but, like the speaker of "I felt a Funeral, in my Brain," the "Freezing persons" lapse, in their serial motion, into unconsciousness instead of attaining a conclusive *terminus ad quem.*[11] The ambiguous "outliving" of threatened snow-death—if one attains it—is involuntary.

It might seem that no worse fate could befall thinking than to "finish knowing" or concede to a "letting go" of consciousness; but there is a worse mode of mental life, and that is to "continue knowing," but in a horrible new way. This conception demands a poetic structure that does not end in a final state, whether of static "wreck" or of obliteration of consciousness in "letting go." Thus in

"The first Day's Night had come –," the soul, after surviving a rupture imagined as "a thing so terrible" it goes unnamed, stoically begins to mend her "snapt" strings so as to sing again. A further development then occurs, as a second "horror" arrives with a characteristically sequential *and then:*

> And then – a Day as huge
> As Yesterdays in pairs,
> Unrolled its horror in my face –
> Until it blocked my eyes –
>
> My Brain – begun to laugh –
> I mumbled – like a fool –
> And tho' 'tis Years ago – that Day –
> My Brain keeps giggling – still.
>
> [423; 1862]

A Brain that "keeps giggling – still" would be grateful to have been allowed to "finish knowing" or to "let go," but instead finds itself being tortured by a new form of consciousness, in which intelligible sequence has been replaced by pure nonsequential vibration, without even the sequential steps of the circular round of "After great pain." "Giggling" is noise without articulation, cry wrenched out of its proper grief. It is a form of thought because it issues from the "Brain"—but it has despaired of comprehension. Hysteria as a form of thought—the continual oscillatory vibration that Dickinson names "giggling"—must eventually altogether undo sequence, which is the mark of rationality and advancing life. It undoes chromaticism, too, since "giggling" registers no difference between stages of experience, but responds to each identically.

For the rest of her life, Dickinson alternates between an obliterative posthumousness that "lets go" and a stance that allows some form of continuing life. She is fertile in thinking up ways to be posthumous that can still include chromatic sequence, going so far as to run her cinema backward, smuggling sequential reversal even

into the grave. Frightened of imagining the immobile future of a
corpse, she imagines instead—in a macabre imitation of the chro-
matic steps of creation—resurrecting the dead body, giving it "mo-
tion" backward into life:

> Oh give it motion – deck it sweet
> With Artery and Vein –
> Upon its fastened Lips lay words –
> Affiance it again
> To that Pink stranger we call Dust
> Acquainted more with that
> Than with this horizontal one
> That will not lift its Hat.
>
> [1550; 1881]

This late poem shows what a strong hold chromatic sequence re-
tained on Dickinson's imagination; she would rather run sequence
backward in fantasy than lose it altogether.[12]

In spite of such evasions, death—being "Gathered into the
Earth, / And out of story –" [1398; 1876]—makes sequence mean-
ingless. The only structure suitable to an existence in which one
has "Dropped the Loop / to Past or Period –" is the invariant pres-
ent tense adumbrated in "After great pain"; and it is to this form,
once she has given up on seriality, that Dickinson turns more and
more. But present tenses are many, and commentators have not al-
ways distinguished among them. The present tense of stasis can be
seen not only in the part of "After great pain" that precedes the
"freezing" coda, but also in "The Bone that has no Marrow," in
which a "finished Creature" who has lost her emotional pith exists
solely in the arid present of two verbs, *is* and *has,* relieved only by a
trapped future-tense query which attempts to find a *terminus ad
quem* by alluding to the figure of Nicodemus, who asked Jesus
whether a man can be born again:

> The Bone that has no Marrow,
> What Ultimate for that?

It is not fit for Table
For Beggar or for Cat –

A Bone has obligations –
A Being has the same –
A Marrowless Assembly
Is culpabler than shame –

But how shall finished Creatures
A function fresh obtain?
Old Nicodemus' Phantom
Confronting us again!

[1218; 1871]

The intrinsic hopelessness of this "plot" to change the speaker's marrowless life is summed up and dismissed in the alliterative sequence "Finished: function fresh? Phantom!" Nicodemus's question, so serious in the poetry of Henry Vaughan that Dickinson knew,[13] appears here as part of a folk tale not entirely dismissible, but not efficaciously redemptive. The nonchromatic existence of *has* and *is* will go on without end.

But dearer to Dickinson's thinking, after catastrophe, than the present tense of routine, of *is* and *has,* is the philosophical present tense (an "eternal" present, and therefore not a true tense) appearing in axiom and definition. The poet's attraction to abstraction produces a notable group of "philosophical" poems; but what sort of thinking do we find in them? And how is this "philosophical" tenseless thinking related to the chromatic sequential thinking which for Dickinson's mind had been so necessary and so compulsive that she imagined temporal step-by-step chromaticism as the essential mechanism of nature? (See not only the lyric on sunrise but also such fundamental poems as "Crumbling is not an instant's Act" [1010; 1865].)[14] It is useful, in assessing the relation of chronological thinking to untensed thinking, to compare two poems, one tensed and one untensed, that employ the same metaphor—that of a person who has become blind because of the putting out of eyes (an image that Dickinson may have drawn from her own increasing eye trouble, or from *King Lear,* or both).

The tensed poem, "Before I got my eye put out," shows Dickinson struggling with the post-rupture reduction of the multiple time-zones of "normal" life into a crucial two: Before and After. The poem, spoken from a single "now," looks before and after, purporting to be willing to refuse the remembered glories of seeing (even were they to be re-granted) in order to remain perpetually safe from the known power over the human eye of the burning and blinding Sun:

> Before I got my eye put out –
> I liked as well to see
> As other creatures, that have eyes –
> And know no other way –
>
> But were it told to me, Today,
> That I might have the Sky
> For mine, I tell you that my Heart
> Would split, for size of me –
>
> The Meadows – mine –
> The Mountains – mine –
> All Forests – Stintless stars –
> As much of noon, as I could take –
> Between my finite eyes –
>
> The Motions of the Dipping Birds –
> The Lightning's jointed Road –
> For mine – to look at when I liked,
> The news would strike me dead –
>
> So safer – guess – with just my soul
> Upon the window pane
> Where other creatures put their eyes –
> Incautious – of the Sun –
>   [336; 1862]

The tenses are jumbled here because untroubled chromatic se-
quence has been abrogated by the maiming event: when one dire
disaster looms larger than everything else in life, all other moments
must be crowded into the two bare categories, "Before" and "Af-
ter." They can no longer appear in the *and then's* of even sequenc-
ing. Written serially, the poem would first describe the pastoral
idyll of "Before," then pass through the catastrophe of blinding,
and conclude with the present averred preference for blindness.
But in her intent to make the emotional climax determine the se-
quencing of the plot (since it generated the poem), Dickinson now
puts the middle blinding first. Catastrophe takes pride of place, oc-
cupying the first line of the poem. And the closing stanza does not
end with the victim's present fate where the poem began; rather, it
prophesies that the same fate will fall on a host of other "incau-
tious" creatures, creating an infinitely repeatable sequence of iden-
tical events. This structure removes the uniqueness of the speaker's
own chronologically unfolding fate, subsuming it under the stasis
of, in the first place, permanent personal catastrophe, and, in the
second place, iterative plural form in others.

When Dickinson "rewrites" this poem "philosophically," it is no
longer tensed: it has turned into an "abstract" or "impersonal"
poem, a definition of Renunciation in which the speaker no longer
asserts that the Sun, to which she had incautiously exposed herself,
put her eye out. Rather, she says (universalizing her case), we do
not have our eye put out, but the will puts its own eyes out, at sun-
rise, so as not to allow the glory of the earthly sun to blind it to the
glory of the Creator. The Christian apocalypse—the "uncovered"
vision of revelation—provides Dickinson with her metaphor moti-
vating erotic renunciation:

> Renunciation – is a piercing Virtue –
> The letting go
> A Presence – for an Expectation –
> Not now –

The putting out of Eyes –
Just Sunrise –
Lest Day –
Day's Great Progenitor –
Outvie
Renunciation – is the Choosing
Against itself –
Itself to justify
Unto itself –
When larger function –
Make that appear –
Smaller – that covered Vision – Here –

[782; 1863]

Dickinson surrounds the central event of self-blinding with many implied tenses: there was the brief moment of sunrise, then the moment when the will (spurred on by that "piercing" virtue, Renunciation) put out its eyes so as not to see Day; there had been a smaller "covered Vision" here, before the self-mutilation, but there will be a larger apocalyptic ("uncovered") Vision hereafter. Yet all of these moments—which were tensed in "Before I got my eye put out"—have in this rewriting been crowded into a single definitional "now" and "here." Dickinson turns the events into gerunds ("The letting go / A Presence," "The putting out of Eyes," "the Choosing") and appends—to end suspense—a final clause that motivates the gerunds: the will does these things when an envisaged "larger" function makes that covered Vision here appear smaller. The definitional frame ("Renunciation is") and the "eternal" present tense of philosophical utterance support the apodictic certainty of Dickinson's propositions here.

But, we must ask, why does Dickinson, normally so intent on compression, proffer in this poem a *double* definition of Renunciation, giving the poem the formal structure of reprise? She has written—if we regularize the poem—two eight-line stanzas, of which

the first formulates a complete definition of Renunciation in the
first-order terms of natural Sunrise, natural eyes, and their Great
Progenitor (a Miltonic version of God). Why, then, does Dickinson
feel that she must add to this metaphorical definition (which has
employed, if in altered form, the metaphor of mutilation bor-
rowed from "Before I got my eye put out") an additional stanza,
defining Renunciation in the second-order religious diction of
choice, justification, and Vision? The new second-stanza discourse
has "cancelled out" Nature (sun, eyes) in favor of an almost mathe-
matical formulation of renunciatory choice: "Renunciation is the
[will's] choosing against itself to justify itself unto itself." The word
in this stanza that belongs to neither natural nor theological dis-
course is "function"—a word more scientific and algebraic[15] than
we might have expected in this context had we not seen the strict
mathematics of the self, which is allied (through the word "func-
tion") with the larger mathematics of the universe.

The splitting of the self by which the voluntary self chooses
against its erotic self in order to justify its existential self to its spiri-
tual self (so I unfold the phrases) is conveyed in a dry untensed
analysis of moral anguish, stemming from the belief in a "larger
function" which the will must respect. The devoting of the second
stanza to the abstract function of choice, rather than to the earlier
first-order metaphorical drama of self-mutilation, shows Dickin-
son's ultimate allegiance, in moral questions, to the most skeletal
and schematic form of thought. And the revision here of the meta-
phor of mutilation borrowed from "Before I got my eye put out"—
now revealing that the blindness was self-inflicted rather than ex-
ternally imposed—suggests Dickinson's habitual intellectual inter-
rogation of formulations she had employed before.[16] The previous
poem's formula of self as victim has been replaced by the formula
of self as deliberate moral agent; the formula of gothic torture-
melodrama has been replaced by a severe minimalist analysis; two
former Dickinsonian forms of tensed narration—the one of serial
chromatic unfolding, and the one that foregrounds climax flanked
by Before and After rather than seriality once existence has defini-

tively been broken in two—have been replaced in "Renunciation" by the tenseless absolutes of confirmed decision.

As Dickinson comes to realize the extent to which she has willed her own deprivation, she explores further and further the paradox by which, for her, the desired object would cease to be compelling once it had been obtained. In consequence, her verse becomes less narrative, less bound to sequence and its termini, and more philosophical. The involuntary stasis of the "giggling" loosened brain has been superseded; now the brain, in a stasis which is philosophical and voluntary, estimates, measures, and weighs experience in the scales of a hypothesized, if unprovable, eternity. Dickinson's gothic playlet imagining her own posthumousness fades (though it never disappears) in favor of looking on things from "God's" vantage point, in which time does not exist, and life and death are seen under the rubric of eternal moral truth.[17]

There is a falling off in Dickinson's verse in the latter years of her life, a regression, sometimes, to earlier and easier formulations. Yet she continues to perfect, in addition to her present-tense poems of a philosophical eternity, poems with a gnomic mixture of tenses within a single complex formulation clustered around a catastrophe. She composes, for instance, a single-quatrain poem about having said a normal goodbye one day to a person who, shortly afterward, died. Written out in prose, the sentiment would read: "How infinite would the encounter be if we suspected—as we cannot ever do—that that recent casual interview would be marked by us, afterwards, as the last time we were to see that person." Dickinson's epigram of cognitive impossibility indulges ironically in a tense-play and mood-play on the verb *to be,* the verb of existence no sooner invoked than extinguished—*Were it to be; would be; was:*

> Were it to be the last
> How infinite would be
> What we did not suspect was marked
> Our final interview.
> [1165; 1870][18]

Moments such as these, which focus on life's unavoidable temporal contingency, render nugatory the confident eternal-present definitions (as in "Renunciation") so attractive to Dickinson as a way out of uncertainty. No axioms and no definitions can cover over a moment of remorse such as that enacted by this little multimodal quatrain of hindsight. Dickinson's attraction to philosophical axioms as escapes from seriality always wrestles, in her later work, with a realist subjugation to change and "experiment." On the one hand, we are told of the final superiority of the Platonic Forms of thought:

> For Pattern is the mind bestowed
> That imitating her
> Our most ignoble services
> Exhibit worthier –
>> ["Who goes to dine must take
>> his Feast"; 1219; 1871]

On the other hand, we hear of the final superiority of sequential pragmatic discovery, capable always of overthrowing our axioms even before we can enunciate them:

> Experiment escorts us last –
> His pungent company
> Will not allow an Axiom
> An Opportunity –
>> [1181; 1870]

If we review the structures of temporality invented over her lifetime by Dickinson to enact her reflections on how human experience can be adequately represented, we see that the poems originally assumed the "normal" presumption that life is essentially a seamless narrative with a beginning, an extended middle, and an end. This view is expressed not only by pleasant "chromatic" poems such as "I like to see it lap the Miles –" but also—as the poet becomes aware that life has no foreseeable or neat ending—in such fearful "chromatic" poems as "The Heart asks Pleasure – first –" or "Because I could not stop for Death –." Unable to think any longer that endings are either predictable or pleasant, Dickinson writes poems that baffle closural arrest:

> Since then – 'tis Centuries – and yet
> Feels shorter than the Day
> I first surmised the Horses' Heads
> Were toward Eternity –
>> ["Because I could not stop for
>> Death –"; 479; 1862]

Eventually, the anxiety-allaying view of life as an evenly incremental series of events is shattered by an event too overwhelming to be assimilated within a chromatic series. The crack, fissure, trough, or abyss most famously present in the moment when "a Plank in Reason, broke," is less violently but quite as desolately phrased in the poem "I cannot live with You –" as "just the Door ajar / That Oceans are –" [706; 1863].

Even after the catastrophic event, Dickinson sometimes attempts to hold on to a chromatic structure while conforming it to her sense of rupture by making *every* event in a chromatic series a shattering and destructive one. She does this in "The Wind begun to knead the Grass –" [796; 1864–1883, Version C, 1873] in which the successive verbs are chiefly violent and destructive—*rock, threw, unhooked, started, scoop itself, throw away, quickened, hurried, showed, put up, flung, wrecked, quartering*—and even the verbs (such as *showed*) that in isolation might seem neutral, in context are made menacing ("The Lightning showed a Yellow Beak / And then a livid Claw –"). Adopting such an invariant thought-grid—one determined to register nothing but cruel blows—satisfied Dickinson's sense of crisis, but not her sense of truth.

As the years go on, and Dickinson changes her thinking on the adequate temporal shape by which to mirror life, she tends to put aside a chromatic slot-filled structuring in favor of other forms. As we have seen, in one such shape the mind sorts its serial experience into two receptacles, "Before" and "After"; in a second, thought concedes to unconsciousness before a terminus is attained; in a third, a hysterical iterative "giggling" prevails, preventing any differentiating chromaticism and eventual termination; in a fourth, a present-tense dead indifference, governed by repetitive apathetic *or*'s, is substituted for active living; in a fifth, Dickinson urges experience into an eternal present-tense or infinitive form that becomes symbolic of the mind's philosophical mastery over incomprehensible seriality; and in a sixth, the serial unfolding consists solely of one catastrophe after another.

Another, and more complex, form adopted by Dickinson after catastrophe is a disarranging of normal serial plot-positions in favor of ranking events according to their importance in an emotional hierarchy. I distinguish this from the binary "Before" and "After" plot because there are usually more incremental steps in these narratives of disarranged plot. In them, beginning may be placed not at the beginning, but at the end; or ending—as we have seen in "Before I got my eye put out"—may replace beginning at the very opening of the poem. The most famous early example of this restructuring of serial experience into a nonsequential arrangement occurs in "There's a certain Slant of light" [320; 1862]. We begin *in medias res,* with the light already present, and without any orienting introduction (such as "I'll tell you how the Sun rose"):

> There's a certain Slant of light,
> Winter Afternoons –
> That oppresses, like the Heft
> Of Cathedral Tunes –

Because the mysterious oppression offered by the light requires interpretation, the "normal" serial and chromatic progression of the

day, ribbon by ribbon, to darkness is interrupted for reflection. An-
alyzing the light-inflicted oppression, Dickinson reveals its emo-
tional name ("Hurt"), its allegorical name ("Despair"), and its im-
perial origin ("of the Air"):

> Heavenly Hurt, it gives us –
> We can find no scar,
> But internal difference –
> Where the Meanings, are –
>
> None may teach it – Any –
> 'Tis the Seal Despair –
> An imperial affliction
> Sent us of the Air –

Only after this full interpretation does the speaker hurry to a quick
and nonchromatic narrative ending, in which the temporal plot of
the brief light is deprived of all middle extension, and is allowed
only a coming and a going. The arrival of the strange afternoon
light (which in a chronologically arranged poem would have been
mentioned at the beginning) is conveyed in terms of the reactions
to it of its personified double audience—the surrounding land-
scape and the shadows that find themselves lengthening in the
oblique light:

> When it comes, the Landscape listens –
> Shadows – hold their breath –

The entire oddity of this, as the verbs enunciating responses to *light*
turn out, anomalously, to be *listen* and *hold* (one's breath)—where
we might expect, for instance, *watch* and *behold*—marks the light's
function as presentiment. Someone is coming for whose dreaded
step the Landscape listens; an event is imminent that will befall the
Shadows before they can again draw breath.

The going of the light, by contrast, abolishes in darkness both

the landscape and the individual shadows. The light itself is irre-
trievable; and with its departure a great horizontal distance re-
places the slanted verticality which, if it is not entirely the perpen-
dicular we associate with transcendence, still originally drew the
eyes to the light:

> When it goes, 'tis like the Distance
> On the look of Death –

Dickinson's structure in "There's a certain Slant of light" opens
with no personal beginning (such as "I like to see it" or "I'll tell
you"), interrupts the expected plot of day's decline with allegorical
interpretation, and ends with the briefest of glances in which plot
is reduced to an arrival—"When it comes"—and a departure—
"When it goes." The coming and going are folded into a single
final epigrammatic and summarizing stanza. Dickinson has here in-
vented a form that allows a conflation of the timeless philosophi-
cal order of defining and allegorizing ("There's a certain Slant of
light") with the temporal order of experience (*comes* and *goes*). But
the temporal order has been cruelly shrunk to a subordinate (if cli-
mactic) position in the drama of thought, and, by reducing it to be-
ginning and end alone, with no middle extension, Dickinson has
abolished almost entirely the linear chromatic sense of existence.[19]

The most famous of the posthumously-voiced poems—"I heard
a Fly buzz – when I died –"—makes a comparable, but blasphe-
mous, change in what "should have been" a "normal" chromatic
step-by-step exhaustive narrative of Christian dying. "I heard a Fly
buzz –" "ought" to begin with its second line, and follow the ex-
pected ritual order of the Christian "happy death": the room is still;
the bystanders have wept themselves silent; the dying one has
made a will; the last onset of Death is felt in the "gathering" of
breaths; and then the expected King comes to lead his redeemed
subject home. Instead of the King, in Dickinson's poem, there
comes a Fly. But the Fly does not appear merely at the crucial link

in the serial order, the moment when the King should appear. In-
stead, the Fly—who provides the ironic final sense-experience of
the speaker before her eyes fail—comes *first*, as Dickinson boldly
inverts the *terminus ad quem* of seriality into the *terminus a quo* of
importance. And then the Fly of fleshly corruption comes *again*,
rudely "interpos[ing]" himself in the very place, and at the very
"slot" in the chromatic story, where the King ought to be:

> I heard a Fly buzz – when I died –
> The Stillness in the Room
> Was like the Stillness in the Air –
> Between the Heaves of Storm –
>
> The Eyes around – had wrung them dry –
> And Breaths were gathering firm
> For that last Onset – when the King
> Be witnessed – in the Room –
>
> I willed my Keepsakes – Signed away
> What portion of me be
> Assignable – and then it was
> There interposed a Fly –
>
> With Blue – uncertain – stumbling Buzz –
> Between the light – and me –
> And then the Windows failed – and then
> I could not see to see –
>
> [591; 1863]

The speaker's closing fall into unconsciousness ("I could not see to
see") is familiar from poems such as "I felt a Funeral, in my Brain"
("And Finished knowing – then –"), but those poems had main-
tained, if with difficulty, the chromatic, step-by-step order of the
recounted experience (the enacting, for example, of the funeral rit-
ual). The Fly pushes that order aside, insisting on his preeminence

in the tale. The chromatic and serial unfolding of experience here yields to the constructing of experience according to the order of momentousness; and the Fly, in his power to insist on his gross material finality of color and sound, his "Blue – uncertain – stumbling Buzz –," is more momentous than the expected, but treacherously absent, King.

Even though, in "I heard a Fly buzz –," beginning and end are one, time still does manifest a terminus in the form of death. In later years, Dickinson would imagine predicaments in which the soul is stalled altogether and narrative cannot proceed to any ending at all. Some lives, she reflects, never had even a beginning, nor an expansion, nor a terminus.[20] Or she would reflect the inconsistency of temporal perception in the mind by averring, in a single poem, that Pain is both immeasurably long, capable of infinite serial chromaticisms, and infinitely short, contracting seriality into a vanishing point. The first stanza of the 1864 poem "Pain – expands the Time –" constructs Pain in terms of something like the strings of contemporary physics, where "Ages" (of infinite potential dimension) lie coiled in a single brain; but the second stanza constructs Pain as something like the hypothesized moment before the Big Bang, when a single second—in human terms, the second of the bullet of feeling that inflicts a mortal wound—contains all of the emotional universe:

> Pain – expands the Time –
> Ages coil within
> The minute Circumference
> Of a single Brain –
>
> Pain contracts – the Time –
> Occupied with Shot
> Gammuts of Eternities
> Are as they were not –
> [833; 1864]

Nobody who has begun to think of time in this topological and malleable fashion could ever entirely believe again in a steady-stepping serial poem. Although the order of emotionally evaluative thought can yield, as in this poem, logically incompatible assertions, Dickinson is unwilling to abandon the conclusive formulations of philosophical eternal present-tense thought—Pain expands the Time; Pain contracts the Time—even when her propositions contradict each other. Rather than write two poems—one of the Pain that expands Time, and one of the Pain that contracts it—she ruthlessly incorporates both "truths" into one poem, making the principle of paradoxical contradiction itself into the truth-value asserted by her stanzas.

Dickinson initially constructs her poetic structures to suggest a view of existence experienced intelligibly, serially, and chromatically, whether in delight or apprehension. She then modifies her structures to show seriality mutating into iterative stasis as others repeat her fate; or to suggest serial hope deliquescing into uncertain termini or no termini at all; or to shrink her original leisured seriality to three points ("Born – Bridalled – Shrouded") or even to two ("When it comes . . . When it goes"); or to reflect a serial oscillatory "giggling" hysteria without terminus; or to arrange life in a seriality of uninterrupted catastrophe; or to reduce chromatic seriality into the crisis-terms of Before and After catastrophe; or to abort plot and wrest incipits and termini out of their normal place; or to think in a "regardless" indifference of circular *or*'s instead of even a purposeless *and then;* or to formulate "eternal" truths in a metaphysical evaluative order that might rise above seriality and termini; or to think topologically until seriality expands to Ages (however compressed) or contracts to a point that extirpates eternities. By thinking through such models of temporality, by constructing so many versions, evasions, and revisions of the seriality that was her original defense against anxiety, Dickinson makes us conscious of the extent to which examining a poet's intellectual models of experience is indispensable to the understanding of art.

4

W. B. Yeats Thinking

THINKING IN IMAGES, THINKING IN ASSERTIONS

> Seek those images
> That constitute the wild;
> The lion and the virgin,
> The harlot and the child.
>
> From "Those Images" (1937)[1]

A POET'S COMPOSITIONAL THINKING becomes increasingly complicated when the experiences and imaginative discoveries of past decades have to be folded into the work of the present. In writing *A Vision,* Yeats reflected on how the salient events in one's life might retrospectively be given intellectual order, imagining an afterlife in which one would construct different schemes of arrangement of those events. One might relive one's life purely chronologically, reviewing it in the form of images unscrolling themselves in their original sequence. Or one might scroll those images backwards, finally understanding the earlier events (as one could not at the time) as foretastes and causes of later ones. Or one might order the significant events and images of one's life in a hierarchy, with the most emotionally decisive ones at the top, and so on down the ladder. In writing his late retrospective poetry, Yeats plays in comparable ways with the ordering of images; and once he has found and settled on a plan of arrangement for his significant images, the poem "clicks" into place.

But images are not easily found—and Yeats's habit of thinking in images requires images to think with. When he cannot find the image he needs, he must, frustratedly, resort to discursive statement until the previously unacknowledged emotional and imaginative impulses burst forth in images so violent as to be undeniable. We can track Yeats's thinking by investigating his arrangement of images; and I will consider, as examples of this characteristic Yeatsian process, two late retrospective poems written in *ottava rima*— "Among School Children," written in 1926 on the day after Yeats's sixty-first birthday, and "The Circus Animals' Desertion," written in 1937 or 1938 when Yeats was seventy-two or seventy-three. He was to die at the beginning of 1939.

Yeats's images usually appear to him in the form of Blakean antinomies or opposites. They structure Yeats's work in Heraclitean fashion, as they die each other's life, live each other's death. But the nature of such antinomies is intensely queried in the later work. In the retrospective work, above all, they take on strange composite forms. "Among School Children" (*Variorum Edition*, 443–446), with which I begin, is Yeats's most harrowing investigation, by means of images, of the worth of his antinomies as a mental principle of order; "The Circus Animals' Desertion" (629–630), with which I end, no longer finds the antinomy of life and art a valid structure for generating images. I have chosen the much-discussed "Among School Children" because it is so nakedly structured by images, and is also resolved by an image. In writing this poem Yeats, as I see it, arranges his images in several antithetical diptychs, and then layers those different diptychs one upon another until they form a single dense palimpsest. Although the poem appears to end with yet one more diptych, as Yeats juxtaposes the blossoming chestnut tree and the self-choreographing dancer, in fact these two images, as I hope to show, do not create a diptych, but are singular and freestanding proposals, repeating a final, divergent, act of thinking.

Among School Children

I

I walk through the long schoolroom questioning;
A kind old nun in a white hood replies;
The children learn to cipher and to sing,
To study reading-books and history,
To cut and sew, be neat in everything
In the best modern way—the children's eyes
In momentary wonder stare upon
A sixty-year-old smiling public man.

II

I dream of a Ledaean body, bent
Above a sinking fire, a tale that she
Told of a harsh reproof, or trivial event
That changed some childish day to tragedy—
Told, and it seemed that our two natures blent
Into a sphere from youthful sympathy,
Or else, to alter Plato's parable,
Into the yolk and white of the one shell.

III

And thinking of that fit of grief or rage
I look upon one child or t'other there
And wonder if she stood so at that age—
For even daughters of the swan can share
Something of every paddler's heritage—
And had that colour upon cheek or hair,
And thereupon my heart is driven wild:
She stands before me as a living child.

IV

Her present image floats into the mind—
Did Quattrocento finger fashion it
Hollow of cheek as though it drank the wind

And took a mess of shadows for its meat?
And I though never of Ledaean kind
Had pretty plumage once—enough of that,
Better to smile on all that smile, and show
There is a comfortable kind of old scarecrow.

V

What youthful mother, a shape upon her lap
Honey of generation had betrayed,
And that must sleep, shriek, struggle to escape
As recollection or the drug decide,
Would think her son, did she but see that shape
With sixty or more winters on its head,
A compensation for the pang of his birth,
Or the uncertainty of his setting forth?

VI

Plato thought nature but a spume that plays
Upon a ghostly paradigm of things;
Solider Aristotle played the taws
Upon the bottom of a king of kings;
World-famous golden-thighed Pythagoras
Fingered upon a fiddle-stick or strings
What a star sang and careless Muses heard:
Old clothes upon old sticks to scare a bird.

VII

Both nuns and mothers worship images,
But those the candles light are not as those
That animate a mother's reveries,
But keep a marble or a bronze repose.
And yet they too break hearts—O Presences
That passion, piety or affection knows,
And that all heavenly glory symbolise—
O self-born mockers of man's enterprise;

VIII

Labour is blossoming or dancing where
The body is not bruised to pleasure soul,
Nor beauty born out of its own despair,
Nor blear-eyed wisdom out of midnight oil.
O chestnut-tree, great-rooted blossomer,
Are you the leaf, the blossom, or the bole?
O body swayed to music, O brightening glance,
How can we know the dancer from the dance?

The plot of "Among School Children" is well known. Yeats, the sixty-year-old Anglo-Irish senator, is visiting a Montessori school staffed by nuns. He is expected to play, to the nun-teacher, the role of interested questioner; to the children, the role of "smiling public man." Bored by the whole programmed scene, the poet lets his mind wander, thinking about himself and his beloved Maud Gonne, whom he has always associated with Helen of Troy, the twin daughter—along with Clytemnestra—of Leda and Zeus (appearing in the form of a swan). Remembering Plato's myth that we were, before our descent into generation, spheres united to our opposite half, the poet rephrases the myth away from Zeus's assault and toward Leda's twin-containing egg: he and Maud, in their youth, as she confided in him about a day of childish tragedy, seemed blended by sympathy "into the yolk and white of the one shell." The sight of the children in the classroom makes the poet wonder if any one of them resembles Maud when she was their age, before he knew her. Feeling a momentary disloyalty to Maud in comparing her to these ordinary children, he justifies the comparison by recalling the tale of the Ugly Duckling, saying parenthetically that even though his Ledaean beloved was to grow up to be a swan, she might well in childhood have resembled one of the ordinary "paddlers" of this classroom. He then remembers, with a pang, that she is now as old as he. The poem proceeds to generalize the decline seen in his and Maud's aging, asking whether any mother, if she could see her son at sixty (his own present age), would think it worthwhile to have borne him. The poet, looking on children beginning their instruction in school, also notes the incapacity of knowledge to prevent bodily decline: even the best philosophers, whatever their hard-won theory of being—otherworldly in Plato, material in Aristotle, or aesthetic in Pythagoras—become in the end merely old scarecrows like the poet himself. As the poem approaches the end of its narrative, it summarizes, with anger, its organizing antinomies, wishing for some utopia where human aspiration—in nuns, in lovers, in mothers, in philosophers—would not come to such a blighted fate:

> Labour is blossoming or dancing where
> The body is not bruised to pleasure soul,
> Nor beauty born out of its own despair,
> Nor blear-eyed wisdom out of midnight oil.

The antinomies here are labor versus spontaneous blossoming or voluntary dancing, mortified body versus erotic body, beauty versus the despair it occasions in its frustrated worshipper,[2] and an effortless wisdom versus the scholar's ruined eyes. The perennial dualism of Western philosophy underlies these conventional oppositions. As we look back through the poem we can find it reiterating these and other antinomies (the young versus the old, religious celibacy versus sexual life, Platonic pre-existence versus biological life, and so on). It is not with the summoning of such conventional oppositions that the active thinking of the poet is engaged. Where, then, will we find it?

Although "Among School Children" begins as a narrative ("I walk"), it changes genres as it proceeds, becoming next a meditative poem ("I dream"), then an ode. We recognize an ode by its address to a divinity, characteristically expressed by a vertically directed "O thou" and by an elevation of tone proper to sublimity. The gods addressed by "Among School Children" in its odal move are the "Presences" that symbolize for us all that heavenly glory might mean. For the lover, the Presence is the idealized image of a permanent beloved; for the nun, her idealized divine personages symbolized by the images in her chapel; for the mother, the idealized image of her perfect son. In the cry that elevates the poem to an ode—"O Presences"—the Presences worshipped by the lover, nun, and mother are named as those generated by human "passion, piety or affection," and are bitterly denominated the heartbreaking "self-born mockers of man's enterprise." This sentiment in itself, too, is a familiar one, and is not the production of the poet's active thinking: it is not to poetry that we need to go to be told that all human worship is doomed to disappointment and defeat, and that we ourselves create that defeat by ascribing more-than-human worth to our idealized love-objects, who in time must reveal the fallibility of their actual being. It is in Yeats's manner that we will find his renewal of the received ideas underlying his poem.

If neither the frame-narrative in the classroom, nor the meditation on aging as producer of scarecrows, nor the odal cry of betrayal represents the thinking-by-images to which I have been referring, what does? Yeats's thinking is visible, first of all, in the serial modulations of genre (at which he is expert), each reflecting his sense that his thinking needs to express itself in a new realm of discourse. Narrative conventionally represents what is going on in the external "real world" of public life (here, the school); meditation, that which is taking place in the private mind of the poet; and the ode—a choral form—that which is true of collective emotional life. Although many poems juxtapose the narrative and the meditative, the odal turn tells us that Yeats intends this poem to reach beyond his public senatorial life and his private situation as a disappointed lover and thinker to a universal truth. He will do this by means of finding and arranging images. How is his thinking in this task visible in the poem he produces?

In answering this question, I begin with the stanza form, *ottava rima,* into which Yeats cast seventeen poems, including both

"Among School Children" and my second example, "The Circus Animals' Desertion." The form first arises in Yeats's work in the volume *The Tower* (1928), although it originates in the stimulus to the poet's imagination provided by his 1907 trip to Italy with Lady Gregory. Yeats associates this stanza form, used by Ariosto and Tasso, with an aristocratic culture in which patronage of the arts brought about—in places such as Urbino, Ferrara, and Florence—a supreme cultural moment. Its use in these despairing late poems seems at first, therefore, painfully ironic.

The *ottava rima* stanza consists of two parts: the first, six-line part, the body of the stanza, rhymes alternately—*ababab*. The second, epigrammatic part is a couplet: *cc*. In its normative unfolding, the stanza presents some theme in the first six lines, and then comments on it in the couplet; the two parts are ordinarily separated in thought, marked by punctuation of some sort at the end of line 6. Yet in "Among School Children," Yeats, we observe, sedulously avoids (until the very end) making such a "normal" or "perfect" stanza, resisting the normative form by light commas or enjambment between body and couplet. His very last stanza, however, is "perfect," leading us to think that restlessness has found rest. Surprisingly—in view of its continuously "imperfect" stanzas— "Among School Children," as it ends, presents itself not only as having found its perfect stanzaic norm, but also as being a poem that is "perfect" in proportion (since it contains eight stanzas of eight lines each). The poem does not declare itself as an ode until the 53rd of its 64 lines—very late in its own unfolding. Both the poem's delayed self-revelation as an ode and its delayed self-revelation as "perfect" (a fact actualized only when it stops after its eighth stanza) are in consonance with its delayed intellectual resolution, which is accomplished, breathtakingly, only in the closing couplet of the final stanza. No other great poem that I know completely withholds the solution to its enigmas to such a late point. The poet means us to understand, as we see him thinking up his "imperfect" stanzas leading to a final "perfect" one, his eventually "perfect" poem-length, his mutating genres concluding in an odal emotional collectiveness, and his daringly postponed imagistic "solution," that life is imperfect as it unfolds and yet perfect as it rounds to completion, lofty in its public, private, and collective yearnings and yet persistently, and enigmatically, disappointing until it can be re-evaluated *in extenso*.

A fundamental aspect of the poet's style of thinking is revealed in the general structuring of the poem as a series of six main im-age-diptychs. Each of these diptychs juxtaposes, brutally, an auspi-cious image of inception and a bitter image of conclusion. The an-titheses are crudely exposed: on the left, we see an all-promising youthfulness or maturity of body or mind; on the right, disap-pointed, grotesque, and risible age. Let me briefly present the dip-tychs as we encounter them, italicizing the good and bad:

On the left:	"the *children's* eyes / In momentary wonder stare upon"
On the right:	the self as "A *sixty-year-old smiling public man*."
On the left:	"She stands before me as a *living child*";
On the right:	her emaciated old-age "*present image* floats into the mind."
On the left:	"I though never of Ledaean kind / Had *pretty plumage* once";
On the right:	the present self-image as a "comfortable kind of *old scarecrow*."
On the left:	a "youthful mother" with "*a shape*" (her baby) on her lap;
On the right:	the same "*shape*" "*with sixty or more winters on its head*";
On the left:	the three philosophers in their moment of *intellectual genius;*
On the right:	a second view of them as "*Old clothes upon old sticks to scare a bird.*"
On the left:	the once-adored "*Presences*";
On the right:	the same by their present name, "*mockers.*"

Finally, in the quick harsh mixed conceptual and imagistic diptychs of the closing stanza we see a *bruised body* against a *pleasured soul; beauty* against *despair;* and *wisdom* against ravaged *eyes.*

The poet's thinking has devised this devastating sequence of diptychs in order to present life as he now perceives it in unsparing hindsight—as promising youth always undone by catastrophic age. As Walt Whitman says, looking in a hand mirror at his body and soul in ruin, "Such a result so soon—and from such a beginning!" ("The Hand-Mirror"). The original life-aim implied by Whitman's word "beginning" was one of worthy production, but the word "result" implies causation ending in decay. By Whitman's standard—which has also been that of Yeats to this point—life must be accounted tragic: the body's decline is inevitable, and the desuetude into which all cultural forms must fall—since none of us are now ghostly Platonists, or solider Aristotelians, or aesthetic Pythagoreans—means that like the body, the mind cannot offer any image of progressive improvement or even continued stability. Whitman's "so soon" is conveyed in Yeats by the immediate collapse of youth into ruin, diptych after diptych.

Yeats's bitter diptychs, though presented serially, are contrived so as to assemble themselves ultimately into a densely overwritten palimpsest. Because of their similarities in image or diction, each becomes overlaid on the next. The poet is sixty; the mother is imagined as seeing her son when he is sixty. The Ugly Duckling of Andersen's story grows up into a swan; Maud, as the Ledaean daughter of Zeus, is also a daughter of the swan. The poet (though not a swan) had pretty plumage once (aligning his youth with Maud's and the Ugly Duckling's); the poet is a scarecrow, and so are the philosophers. The lover and the nuns and the mother—so different in apparent choice of life—become identical when aligned as layers in the palimpsest of worshippers of heartbreaking Presences. The schoolchildren setting forth on the path to knowledge, Maud as a schoolgirl, the poet visiting the school, and the philosophers are actors along a single continuum, that of the pursuit of wisdom. The choral unison in which the odal moment is voiced summarizes the fact that the serial diptychs have become a single universal diptych: on the left, worshippers of images; on the right, broken hearts. The cruelty of horizontal melody—of the poem's catastrophic diptychs, one after another—has become the cruelty as well of vertical harmony, as all the diptychs become aligned in a single unifying chord of despair. Such an impregnable structure— of the sequential becoming the harmonic—is the best evidence of the poet's thinking in images as he composes. And what he thinks —as the structure tells us—is that all life-stories (whether of the body, the mind, or the spirit) become in the end one story, an ineluctably tragic one. The lines say this discursively, too; but the theme convinces only through Yeats's thinking of the superimposed diptychs.

I have not mentioned the one image from the past that apparently escapes being brutalized by an immediately-juxtaposed opposite: the moment of intimate youthful sympathy in which, as Maud confides to her lover a tale of a time before he knew her, he feels momentarily restored to his Platonic pre-existent spheric wholeness. This idyllic moment appears to remain untroubled, until we reflect that the sixty-year-old poet and the gothic hollow-of-cheek Maud now exist apart from each other: the youthful sympathy, so passionately recollected, did not last, and lovers, under the late briefly-mentioned rubric of "passion" in the choral stanza, are slipped in among those consigned to heartbreak. This "undoing" of passion turns the youthful passionate moment, so carefully preserved until the penultimate stanza, into tragedy, subjecting it as well to the degeneration visited so cruelly and immediately in the poem on everything else. The poet has hoped that by carefully sequestering in memory at least one unmarred moment, he could exempt it from the ruining of time; but it too succumbs to the ravages of thought, is in fact the first casualty mentioned as the poem mounts to its sublime moment of address, "O Presences / That passion . . . knows."

If, then, the perturbed thinking of the poet has been made evident to us by a restless and continuing violation of stanza-proportion and by mutations of genre; if his oppositional, architectonic thinking has been shown in the structured accumulation of contrasting diptychs; if the aggressiveness of his thinking has been exposed in the cruelty of those successive diptychs; if his bitterness has been further manifest in the eventual superimposing of the serial diptychs one on another in the vertical chord of ruin's palimpsest, in which all enterprises named in the poem come to the same tragic and heartbreaking conclusion; if the shape of one's life— whether one is lover, nun, or mother—is formed in the one iterated mold of self-deception followed by heartbreak, how will the thinking of the poet resolve this harrowing meditation?

I have said that the poem concludes "perfectly": the eighth stanza finds its normative resting place of free-standing sestet and couplet, and the poem becomes a perfect square of eight-by-eight. We are led to believe, by this prosodic repose and this stanzaic perfection set out by the poet and brought to our attention, that there will be a comparable intellectual resolution, and there is. Each of the two concluding metaphors, that of blossoming and that of dancing—embodied in the chestnut tree and the dancer—strives to find a representation of life that does not come down to a precipitous catastrophic result from an aspiring beginning. Only the second of these, as we shall see, succeeds.

The chestnut tree offers a promising organic picture: though it is old (as we know from the fact that it is "great rooted"), its essence is defiantly summoned up in its defining noun: it is a "blossomer." Whatever its age, the tree's perennial function is to put forth blossoms each spring, fulfilling its biological imperative to reproduce. The roots, the bole, and the leaves are all there to help it to be what it is, a "blossomer"—and it will continue to be a blossomer until its death. This is a bounteous image of an organic steady state, answering the poet's self-evidently gnomic question, "Are you the leaf, the blossom, or the bole?" with "I am all of these (and the root too)." However, the image of the tree (for all its resemblance to the human body in trunk, limbs, and crown) is not well suited to human application for Yeats's purposes here. Human beings cannot "blossom" in reproduction every year until they die. And the tree

has no say in its own life and no individuality: its blossoming is di-
rected solely by biology, and its life is indistinguishable from the life
of every other chestnut tree. The image of involuntary organic
blossoming-unto-death is no solution to the two problems life
poses to human beings: to what end human enterprise (Adam's la-
bor), and to what end the heartbreak resulting from faith in the
Presences. The poem, approaching its penultimate line, remains
unresolved, and the poet's thinking, though promisingly new in de-
taching itself from its compulsive ordering-by-colliding-diptychs,
appears misdirected in its first metaphorical image suggesting a
less despairing view of life, when viewed from the perspective of
old age.

Only in substituting for "blossoming" his second metaphorical
image, "Labour is . . . dancing," does Yeats think his way to an im-
age that can "solve" the poem. (In spite of its grammatical parallel-
ism with the dancer-question, the chestnut-question ideationally
belongs with the four lines preceding it, completing the last stan-
za's sestet. It serves, however, by its grammatical likeness to the
dance-question, as a bridge to the poem's concluding "solving"
couplet.) Before I go further, I want to turn to one of Yeats's drafts
for the ending of the poem. The images found in the draft read at
this point,

> O hawthorn tree, in all that gaudy gear,
> Are you it all or did you make it all?
> O dancing couple, glance that mirrors glance,
> How can we know the dancer from the dance?[3]

The probable allusion in the hawthorn's "gaudy gear" is to *Antony
and Cleopatra*—"Let's have one other gaudy night"—showing the
image of the hawthorn tree to be one of sexual fulfillment, for
which it wears its springtime "gaudy gear." And the image of the
"dancing couple" (in which the dance euphemistically represents
sexual intercourse), suffused with personal intimacy in the "glance

that mirrors glance," also decides that the moment of youthful sexual union in romantic love represents (when life is viewed with the hindsight of old age) its only satisfaction. This decision is even an understandable solution, as memory (as we have seen in the poem) recurs nostalgically to an undamaged image of "youthful sympathy," preserving it briefly from temporal erosion. The difficulty with this "solution" is that this memorial exaltation of past love offers no reason to go on living during the second half of life, in which disappointment has, for Yeats, embittered the memory of passion. His thinking, as we see it stalled in this first draft, has not found any reason for living a life in which the erotic capacity of the body is disappearing—a life which he is, after all, leading at the moment of writing, as he turns sixty.

In revising his closing quatrain, Yeats substitutes an aged, yet still blossoming, chestnut tree for the gaudy hawthorn, and finds a better line than the feebly vague, "Are you it all or did you make it all?" But he has not yet solved the problem of the inapplicability of an unconscious and generic perennially-blossoming tree to the self-aware tragedy of individual human enterprise. In erasing the image of a couple with mirroring glances engaged in a sexually fulfilling dance, in substituting for the couple the image of a single ungendered body "swayed to music," Yeats—in the most dramatic moment of poetic thinking in the poem—deletes sexual companionship from his image of the fulfilled life. The body, it is true, has no choice over the music it must continue to dance to: to that extent, it must follow the fate given it by heredity, environment, and historical contingency. On the other hand, this is a dancer who invents, although dancing to the music of time, a constantly changing choreography. Yeats gives the body a "brightening glance" to show us that the dancer's choreography is being personally, originally, and progressively conceived at every step. The dynamic perpetuity residing within words such as "brighten" or "redden" extends in an ever-intensifying indefiniteness, and the present participle is, by its nature, an ever-active part of speech.

The final question, addressed to the "body swayed to music"—
and reiterating the "O thou" recalled from the addresses to the
Presences and the tree—is not a "real" question: at least it is not
asking for practical directions on how to know a dancer from a
dance. It is voicing a final conviction—that the pattern of our life is
not to be judged by juxtaposing its disillusioned end to its auspi-
cious beginning. Nor are human aspirations to be judged by the
heartbreak to which they succumb, defeated. Instead, Yeats rede-
fines selfhood—daringly, in the 63rd line of a 64-line poem—as the
arc we trace moment by moment in our inventive responses to the
unchosen events of our fate. The music of time plays; our eye
brightens; we think of a step, then another, then another; the mu-
sic changes; our eye brightens again, as we find a different step,
then another, then another. Until the music stops, we are still con-
ceiving new steps. We are that arc we make: the dancer is definable
as a self only by the linearly-extended responsive dance invented
over a lifetime. There is no time when the eye cannot brighten
under another stimulus by fate, not until the music stops as the
eye closes. And the choreography must always be, after all, an act
carried out in solitude: no sexual partner can do our life-inventing
for us.

The poet's thinking ends here on the plane of metaphor, by
which it rises above the originating question of the poem: whether
life is definable only in the tragic terms of the cruel diptychs. Yes,
material existence always exhibits a decline in age; but the choreo-
graphed line of developing selfhood may go up or down, across
and over, because it is essentially a virtual line of psychological and
aesthetic and intellectual self-creation rather than a line of physical
event. The meta-life of response can be forever brightening, even
when the embodied enterprises of passion, piety, and affection re-
sult in harrowing diptychs and tragic palimpsests. Because the
poem itself is part of the meta-life of response, it is "perfect" and
can find ultimate stanzaic "rest," even while including, in unsparing

pictorial form, the broken hearts of the nuns, the mothers, the wisdom-seekers, and not least, the lover who speaks the poem. The poem replicates, in its own changes of genre and address, in its variations in stanza-proportions and metaphor, the actual inventive choreography of the dance, guaranteeing its own fidelity to its discovery.

But I cannot end on this consoling note alone, for much in the poem's writing struggles against it—not least the appalling picture of life, derived from Porphyry, that is sketched out in the fifth stanza. We are shapes betrayed into existence by the honey of generation which has seduced our parents into the intercourse that conceived us. Once we are born, having been given the drug of forgetfulness, we are pitched into a life which has only two available phases, to sleep (forgetting our Platonic pre-existence) or to shriek in horror. If we consent to wakeful consciousness combined with the recollection of our former happy state of pre-existence, we have only one response: to shriek at what we perceive life to be and to struggle, fruitlessly, to escape our prison. Something of this wild and tragic view of human life persists, I think, even after Yeats allows us to exit from the poem as the exulting perpetual inventors of our own selfhood. Are we shrieking and struggling to escape, or are we brightening into our next resourceful and beautiful arc of response? The thinking of the poet compels him to present each alternative equally strongly, just as, at the end, he allows the midnight toil of the blear-eyed sage, the frustrated despair of the beauty-creating poet balked of love, and the mortification of the body by Christian ascetics to share the same stanza with the perennially sexual "blossomer" and the ecstatic dancer. It is probably true to say that no great poem leaves us without a lasting sense of its conflicting passions, even if it ends in "perfection," or announces—to cite Milton's most violent work—that "nothing is here for tears." Poetic thinking cannot, and does not, obliterate or disavow the reflections it engages in en route to its arrival at a "solu-

tion." Yeats's discovery of the great importance of the creative con-
tinuity of life—the articulated and extended dance—cannot erase
what he has seen of the shriek of birth and the heartbreak of age.

Ten or eleven years after composing "Among School Children,"
Yeats wrote another retrospective *ottava rima* poem that thinks in
images, "The Circus Animals' Desertion." If the earlier poem was
precipitated by aging, heartbreak, and the specter of sexual impo-
tence, "The Circus Animals' Desertion" was prompted by Yeats's
fear that he could no longer summon and command, as ringmas-
ter, his troop of images: "Those stilted boys, that burnished char-
iot, / Lion and woman and the Lord knows what." In the past,
"Winter and summer till old age began, / My circus animals were
all on show," but now the poet may have to be satisfied, his menag-
erie having deserted him, with his heart. He thinks about what it
would mean not to be able to find images any longer—that is to
say, not to be able to think as a poet. Unlike "Among School
Children," which thinks throughout via images—its multiple dip-
tychs to begin with; its lover, nuns, and mothers to sum up with; its
invisible Presences over all; and its tree and dancer, to close with—
"The Circus Animals' Desertion" is forbidden to think in images
about its present state: the whole point of the opening is to tell us
that the poet's images have slunk away, deserting their master.
How can the poet who thinks in images write without his images?
He is forced to turn to the opposite and less congenial rhetorical
pole, the pole of statement.

The Circus Animals' Desertion
I
I sought a theme and sought for it in vain,
I sought it daily for six weeks or so.
Maybe at last, being but a broken man,
I must be satisfied with my heart, although
Winter and summer till old age began
My circus animals were all on show,

Those stilted boys, that burnished chariot,
Lion and woman and the Lord knows what.

II

What can I but enumerate old themes?
First that sea-rider Oisin led by the nose
Through three enchanted islands, allegorical dreams,
Vain gaiety, vain battle, vain repose,
Themes of the embittered heart, or so it seems,
That might adorn old songs or courtly shows;
But what cared I that set him on to ride,
I, starved for the bosom of his faery bride?

And then a counter-truth filled out its play,
The Countess Cathleen was the name I gave it;
She, pity-crazed, had given her soul away,
But masterful Heaven had intervened to save it.
I thought my dear must her own soul destroy,
So did fanaticism and hate enslave it,
And this brought forth a dream and soon enough
This dream itself had all my thought and love.

And when the Fool and Blind Man stole the bread
Cuchulain fought the ungovernable sea;
Heart-mysteries there, and yet when all is said
It was the dream itself enchanted me:
Character isolated by a deed
To engross the present and dominate memory.
Players and painted stage took all my love,
And not those things that they were emblems of.

III

Those masterful images because complete
Grew in pure mind, but out of what began?
A mound of refuse or the sweepings of a street,
Old kettles, old bottles, and a broken can,

Old iron, old bones, old rags, that raving slut
Who keeps the till. Now that my ladder's gone,
I must lie down where all the ladders start,
In the foul rag-and-bone shop of the heart.

"The Circus Animals' Desertion" is peculiarly structured
through its three Roman numerals. It has a one-stanza overture at
the beginning, a one-stanza coda at the end, and a middle made up
of three stanzas. The overture tells us, in remarkably plain state-
ments, that the poet can no longer write—"I sought a theme and
sought for it in vain / I sought it daily for six weeks or so"; and the
middle stanzas tell us, in equally plain assertions, that in every case,
in the past, the poet was distracted from his ostensible desire—to
represent the life-mysteries of the heart—by the intrinsically liter-
ary compulsions of the fictive "dream" he was creating in his art.

Each of the three middle stanzas describes, in the past tense, a
significant work written by Yeats before he turned forty: these are
The Wanderings of Oisin (1889), a long three-part narrative in which
the hero visits three magical islands; *The Countess Cathleen* (1892), a
play in which Cathleen, although she sells her soul to the devil to
gain bread for the poor, is redeemed because of the goodness of
her motive; and *On Baile's Strand* (1903), a play about Cuchulain,
who dies tragically in madness, fighting the sea, while in a farcical
subplot a Fool and a Blind Man steal bread from the ovens of the
peasants who have left their houses to watch Cuchulain's struggle.
In his reprise, within "The Circus Animals' Desertion," of each of
these works, Yeats insists that although his writing began in "heart-
mysteries," the independent energy of poetic and dramatic cre-
ation soon (and, it appears, "naturally") overwhelmed the originat-
ing life-motive. The reader perceives this iteration of outcome be-
cause of the structural parallels within the three middle stanzas.
The stanzas of "The Circus Animals' Desertion," unlike the stanzas
of "Among School Children," respect the natural structure of the
ottava rima; because they are intended to represent reflection on

the past (rather than the "spontaneous" wandering of present passionate thought) they are not enjambed, wayward, or syntactically surprising. The self-contained closing couplets are used, in these middle stanzas, to insist on the identical outcome of the writing plot, no matter what its original life-motive. Lest the reader miss the fact of this identity, Yeats makes the latter two stanzas of the middle section rhyme their closing couplets on the same word, "love":

> And this brought forth a dream and soon enough
> This dream itself had all my thought and love.

> Players and painted stage took all my love,
> And not those things that they were emblems of.

It is noteworthy how completely "The Circus Animals' Desertion" has depended on bald assertions and bald questions: these are, in reduced form,

> "I sought a theme . . . I sought it daily . . . Maybe I must be satisfied with my heart . . . What can I but enumerate old themes? . . . But what cared I? . . . Then a counter-truth filled out its play, / *The Countess Cathleen* was the name I gave it. . . . This dream itself had all my thought and love . . . It was the dream itself enchanted me . . . Players and painted stage took all my love."

Where can the sought-for poetry of new images be hiding? Or, to put the question another way, where is Yeats's imagination hiding? It takes no particular imagination to announce that the present crisis has occurred because the writer, deserted by his former images, has been seeking a theme in vain; nor does it take imagination to narrate, in plain terms, the iterative story of the writer's past, in which dream and drama had always, in the end, become more powerful in the poet's heart than life-events themselves.

Since Yeats's images have deserted him, he gives us, perforce, a poem of assertion rather than a poem of images. Images are of course present in reminiscence, in the first evocation of the circus animals, but Yeats refers to them with the distant deictic *those* as images no longer useful: "those stilted boys . . . / Lion and woman and the Lord knows what." This image-circus is a thing of the past: the sestet-rhymes, *"vain . . . man . . . began,"* carry the weight of the story. Nor does the middle of the poem invent powerful new images. What Yeats's thinking expends itself on, in the middle stanzas, is manner: finding a different manner of description for each of his three remembered works. The first manner, invented for the description of *The Wanderings of Oisin,* is one of a ferocious and self-lacerating clash of tones, as the poet mystifies and then scornfully demystifies Oisin's journeys. He reiterates, in the thrice-repeated "vain" of that demystification, the "in vain" of the first stanza of "Desertion" itself:

> First, that [daring, heroic, mythical] sea-rider Oisin
> led [the fool!] by the nose
> Through three enchanted [beautiful, magical, mysterious]
> islands, [which were only] allegorical dreams,
> Vain gaiety, vain battle, vain repose.

"Themes . . . dreams . . . seems" run the sestet-rhymes, ringing the death-knell of youthful Yeatsian romance.

The second manner, created for the conveying of *The Countess Cathleen,* is hyperbolic, melodramatic, and gothic: the desperate heroine, "pity-crazed," has been saved from the devil by the intervention of "masterful heaven," as in a medieval romance, but the poet fears that his dear one, Maud, will lose her soul to hatred. The paradox of Cathleen's redemption is played out in Yeats's slightly ironic feminine rhymes: "the name I gave it" represents the dramatic poet's contribution, "save it" stands for heaven's part in the soul-drama, and "enslave it" recalls Maud's endangering of her soul by hate. Although the poet is aware of the black-and-white counters out of which he made his play—God, the Devil, the Saint, and the Lover—he does not here mock his own creation, as he had done in speaking of *Oisin*. In fact, by calling *The Countess Cathleen* "a counter-*truth*," Yeats retrospectively confers truth-value also on *The Wanderings of Oisin*. Yet he remains at a distance from his own early play, and cannot praise it without reservation (though one sees his pride as creator in the naive boast, "the name *I gave* it," the comment linking the *counter*-truth to the *Countess*).

However, when the poet arrives at his third reflection—the one describing *On Baile's Strand*—he introduces a wholly different, and very striking, manner. The play is described not mockingly as a vain allegory, not melodramatically as a religious fable about selling one's soul, but instead soberly, in language appropriate to an Aristotelian tragedy. Yeats's diction draws on the *Poetics*:

Character	[of a heroic kind]
isolated	[singled out for tragic status]
by a deed	[a singular act of, for example, hubris]
to engross	[absorb, fascinate; acquire all of, monopolize; prepare the text of an official document, inscribe in a large hand]
the present	[era] and
dominate	[by being "larger than life"]
memory	[cultural tradition].

Before this point in the poem, Yeats's English (in such phrases as "The Lord knows what," "led by the nose," and "my dear") has allowed itself to be familiar, even slangy. But in this passage he is writing, except for the word *deed,* in pure Latin: *character; isola; ingrossare; praesens; dominare; memoria.* One can almost hear the parallels at the end resonating in monumental Latin: *ingrossare praesentem memoriamque dominare.* If not quite Latin, this passage is at least latinate Yeats, and, by its weight and seriousness and appeal to the *Poetics,* it passes a judgment on his past work that reflects legitimate authorial pride, sanctioned by Greek tragic tradition. The poet has ceased to be dismissive of, or alienated from, his own work. However, this Aristotelian description ("Character isolated by a deed") applies only to Cuchulain; it suppresses the Fool and Blind Man who act out the farce that runs concurrent with Cuchulain's epic deed. A full definition of literature—one that would include "low" dramatis personae as well as high heroes—seems unavailable at this moment to the poet; yet the base motives of the Fool and Blind Man must have been part of the "heart-mysteries" generating the play.

It is in the succinctly different manners of these three descriptions that the Yeatsian stylistic intelligence—held in check in the bald assertions and questions of the stanzas—exerts itself. But it cannot yet create new images. The Yeatsian intelligence is also at work in the creation of the suspense governing the poem: Will the poet find a theme? Will recalling past works prime the pump for the creation of new images? Does the poet truly exist any longer if he is a non-writing writer?

All three aspects of the imaginative strategy of the poem (suspense, bald assertion, mannered styles) converge in the coda. In answer to the suspense: No, the writer has not found a new theme in his old sense of the word—a "heart-mystery" that he can elevate into an imagined narrative about an iconic image with a heroic name: Oisin, Cathleen, Cuchulain. In answer to the bald rhetoric: No, the manner of flat assertion will not give way to something rapt or visionary: the poet will remain on the syntactic plane of naked statement. (The chain of such unadorned assertions beginning with "I sought a theme" and followed by "What can I but enumerate old themes?" is concluded in the coda by "I must lie down.") Finally, in answer to the question whether the poet can find new images of the exalted kind represented by "those *masterful* images" of past works, linked by their adjective to the *masterful* Heaven of supernatural power that saved Cathleen, a baleful and wholly un-exalted image surges up—the image of the poet's present location, his heart, now not a lodge of mystery but a repulsive shop. We are very far from the exquisite "shop" of Shakespeare's sonnet 24, in which the heart contains the painted image of the ideal beloved.[4] Instead, in savage parody of the Renaissance love-tradition, Yeats's heart—in the debased image which has welled up unsought—is a low "rag-and-bone shop," into which the poet has entered from time to time in the past, to ransom some piece of detritus from his life-experience by paying a price to "that raving slut / Who keeps the till." (His Muse is linked to "those" circus animals and "those" past masterful images by *her* adjective of deictic distance, "that.") In the past, the poet has been able (after paying a fee) to climb up a ladder with his retrieved piece of trash, raising it to the heavenly realm of "pure mind," where it can grow into a completed "masterful image." The poem, with this revelation, unmasks itself as one concerned with what Freud called sublimation. The past strategy—to transform the original ransomed "heart-mystery," to coax it to grow in "pure mind" until it became a "masterful image" such as Cuchulain—has become impossible. We understand better, now, the poet's current lack of circus animals: the Muse will not release anything further from her shop for the old Romantic purpose of idealized iconic transformation.

The declaration "Hitherto I have written rhetoric; but now I will look into my heart and write truth" is an old one; every writer aims to show "[le] coeur mis à nu." But the emblematic rendition of the naked heart must be historically rethought from century to century, from Dante on. We have so far been led to think of the heart as something entirely subliterary, since we have heard, in stanza one, Yeats distinguish "heart" from both "theme" and circus-images, and in stanzas three and four, distinguish it from both "dream" and "emblem." What is our surprise when this hitherto imageless poet—one so barrenly confined to assertions and questions—bursts forth, once the past practice of sublimation has been recognized as unworkable in the present, with a shattering cascade

of ten images: "Those masterful images . . . out of what began?"
They came from

> A mound of refuse
>   or
> the sweepings of a street, /
>   Old kettles
>   old bottles,
>   and
>   a broken can, /
>   Old iron,
>   old bones,
>   old rags,
>   that raving slut /
>   Who keeps the till.

A longer analysis of this accumulation would track Yeats's ener-
getic poetic thinking as he adds each image to the heap. The first
nouns ("mound," "sweepings") represent an abstract and undiffer-
entiated mass; then the heaps are sorted into like objects (still us-
able "kettles" and "bottles") as though order needed to be made of
the leftovers of the past (we recall age like "a sort of battered kettle
at the heel" in *The Tower*); this close-focus glimpse of what has
been ordered reminds us of what remains to be done, giving us "a
broken can" (where are further cans that we can bring together
with this one, to make a third ordered heap, called "broken cans"?).
At least kettles and bottles and cans are objects that retain their
outline and integrity; but the next list, as Yeats scrutinizes more
closely the contents of his heart, offers *disjecta membra* of machin-
ery, bodies, and clothes: "iron," "bones," "rags." The poet's exhum-
ing of his past has reached the matter of the grave, and can go no
further, except to give a last look at his Muse. She was Niamh to
his Oisin, she was Cathleen to his Aleel, she was Maeve to his
Cuchulain, but she is now the libidinous id, the erotic and irratio-

nal desire that dwells below all conscious life, "that raving slut / Who keeps the till." The poet who complained that he lacked a theme has found one erupting with a vengeance—and with it a torrent of new images.

As Yeats shows us how his initial distress at sterility and his alienation from past works yield a falling from his ladder of sublimation through the trapdoor of long-maintained repression into the cellar of the "subliterary" heart—which turns out to possess a profusion of images just waiting to be explored—we fully comprehend the strategy of the poem. We have been made to sympathize at first with the depressed poet, deserted by his masterful images (which he affects to scorn, because of their disloyal desertion, as mere "circus animals"). By the end, we understand (with the poet) why no "themes" occur to him: his Muse has revolted against being sublimated once again into a faery bride or a countess—or even into a Celtic hero. She sequesters herself stubbornly in her underground fastness of squalor and farce, where the Fool and the Blind Man came from; and she waits until her poet, cornered, will accept her grim hospitality in her environment of old and disintegrating memories. In 1914 Yeats had written, "I made my song a coat / Covered with embroideries / Out of old mythologies / From heel to throat" ("A Coat"), but grandly claimed that he could do without that coat: "There's more enterprise / In walking naked." Now, close to death, he realizes he will have to walk not boldly naked but in humiliating "old rags." In 1910 he had sung, lifting his glass, "Wine comes in at the mouth / And love comes in at the eye" ("A Drinking Song"), but now the bottles are empty and the can is broken. The sword of Cuchulain has become "old iron," the Fenian heroes are "old bones." Yeats is not even sure whether his memories are a sizable "mound of refuse" or the pitifully sparse "sweepings of a street." A rich vein of interpretation and classification lies before him: the inventory of the shop of the heart is a task for many poems. He will never lack a theme again; but he will lack his old manner of sublimation into dreams and dramas. He must write, for the foreseeable future, couched in the Beckettian room of the mad Muse.

It is of course an illusion that a poem can be written without images, just as it is an illusion that a poem can be written without discursive statement. But a poem can tilt its strategy powerfully in one direction or the other, teaching us, on the one hand, to see its diptychs and palimpsests as a form of thinking—by which I mean the poet's seeing relations among, and then arranging symbols of, the raw data of experience—or teaching us, on the other hand, what poetic "dryness" feels like by showing us a discourse of bare statement and bare interrogation, deprived temporarily of all imagery except that which is bitterly, but in the end proudly, recalled from another time. By flooding the poem, then, with new and unforeseen images at the end of "The Circus Animals' Desertion," Yeats criticizes the sublimated earlier form of poetic thinking that seems to have stranded him within a desiccated, self-scorning, and bald discourse. As he surveys the data of life retrospectively in "Among School Children" and "The Circus Animals' Desertion," Yeats shows us the clearest proof that for him it was indispensable not only to think in images but to arrange chains of images in such a way as to make them become the structural, and revelatory, principle of much of his poetry.

Can we deny the name of "thinking" to the satiric discursive miniatures of Pope, the empathetic reprises of Whitman, the multiple reconceivings of seriality by Dickinson, or the complex architectonic assembling of images by Yeats? The poet's style of thinking, instinctual though it may become in the heat of composition, issues from an extensive repertoire of image-memory and intellectual invention, coupled with an uncanny clairvoyance with respect to emotional experience. The first conceptions of any poet are subject to an intense form of critique either mentally or on paper, in which thinking now takes the form of bringing the original materials up to an exquisite level of verbal accuracy; and this is done in the service of replicating in abstract symbolic structures the structures of emotional experience. In justice to the poets, we must call what they do, in the process of conceiving and completing the finished poem, an intricate form of thinking, even if it means expanding our idea of what thinking is. And if we are to understand a poem, we must reconstruct the anterior thinking that generated its surface, its "visible core." That thinking is always in process, always active. It issues not in axioms, but in pictures of the human mind at work, recalling, evaluating, and structuring experience. The evolving discoveries of the poem—psychological, linguistic, historical, philosophical—are not revealed by a thematic paraphrase of their import. They can be grasped only by our participating in the process they unfold. As we are swung back and forth by Pope's analyses of our middle state, we are made to feel our inner divisions; as we are left catching at vacancy with Whitman's "somewhere," we realize the failing hopes of our own filament-launching; as we are dropped from the funeral coffin with Dickinson, we sense Reason's giving way; as we find ourselves deserted in old age by the serviceable concepts of our middle years, we fear, with Yeats, that a permanent loneliness has set in. We are made to feel these things because the poem has been constructed so as to lead us within and through them. The thinking that has invented such poetic labyrinths is worthy of our attention, respect, and even awe.

Notes

Introduction

1. *The Poems of Emily Dickinson,* Variorum Edition, ed. R. W. Franklin (Cambridge, Mass.: The Belknap Press of Harvard University Press, 1998), no. 1097. In Thomas H. Johnson's edition (1955), the poem is numbered 1063.

2. It is disturbing that even a fellow-poet can suppose that the poems of a "major poet" can exist without "a particle of intellect." This is the absolute conclusion concerning the work of Elizabeth Bishop patronizingly voiced by the poet William Logan in a recent review (*Parnassus* 27 [2004], 144):

> Elizabeth Bishop is now often considered [Lowell's] equal, or even superior. . . . She is, to be sure, charming and endlessly resourceful, a major poet who often pretended to be a minor one, an innocent masquerading as a faux innocent. . . . A reader can nevertheless grow tired of poems with so much charm and not a particle of intellect.

It would take an essay to expatiate on the presence of intellect in Bishop's poems—an intellect meditating on the nature of abstract modernism ("The Monument"), on problems of gender (too many poems to mention, from "The Gentleman of Shalott" to "In the Waiting Room"), on the curious prevalence of the aesthetic at all social levels ("The Filling Station"), on the painful acquisition of knowledge ("At the Fishhouses"), on the nature of home and homelessness ("Crusoe in England"), on the search for existential meaning in the absence of religious belief ("Over 2,000 Illustrations"). William Logan's denial of "a particle of intellect" to such poems suggests that he—like many others reading poetry—has a peculiarly limited conception of what intellect is and how it may manifest itself.

3. In "Self-Portrait in a Convex Mirror." I run the risk here that Words-

worth attached to "minute criticism" in his "Essay upon Epitaphs," but I have also his support for the endeavor of such criticism, one that reveals, by "bringing [poets'] words rigorously to the test of thoughts," which words of the poet survive inspection as ones produced by a distinguished creative intentionality:

> Minute criticism is in its nature irksome, and as commonly practiced in books and conversation, is both irksome and injurious. Yet every mind must occasionally be exercised in this discipline, else it cannot learn the art of bringing words rigorously to the test of thoughts.

Wordsworth's Literary Criticism, ed. Nowell C. Smith (1905), reissued with a preface by Howard Mills (Bristol: Bristol Classical Press, 1980), 120.

4. For my attempts to treat Stevens as something other than a poet versifying ideas, see my *On Extended Wings: Wallace Stevens' Longer Poems* (Cambridge, Mass.: Harvard University Press, 1969) and *Wallace Stevens: Words Chosen out of Desire* (Cambridge, Mass.: Harvard University Press, 1984).

1. Alexander Pope Thinking

1. Pope published the *Essay on Man* in parts over the course of a year: Epistle I in February of 1733, Epistles II and III in March and April of the same year; Epistle IV followed in January of 1734.

2. The panel consisted of Professors Hilary Putnam, Judith Shklar, and Melvin Konner. Only selected papers from the English Institute are published, and these were not. Moreover, the original papers are missing from the English Institute Archive (Box 2) in the Harvard University Archives (as are many other essays by contributors, not all of which were given to the Archives subsequent to delivery). I have not attempted to retrieve the original papers, but I do not believe I misrepresent their conclusions.

George Rousseau's 1972 essay "On Reading Pope," in Peter Dixon, ed., *Writers and Their Background: Alexander Pope* (Ohio University Press, 1972, 1–59), says optimistically that Pope's "mighty themes—virtue, vice, corruption, pride, genuine versus perfunctory art, freedom, the law, to mention a few—are now the perpetual talk of social and natural scientists as well as poets and critics" (3). But it is not by his themes—or discussion of them as such by "social and natural scientists . . . poets and critics"—that a poet lives, but by discussion of the new manner of being and representation that he has elicited from language. As Leopold Damrosch observes in *The Imagina-*

tive World of Alexander Pope (Berkeley: University of California Press, 1987, 139): "If the history of ideas is allowed to treat concepts as primary and lived experience as secondary, then it seriously distorts what it studies." Damrosch quotes Carl Schorske as saying, "Historians had been too long content to use the artifacts of high culture as mere illustrative reflections of political or social developments, or to relativize them to ideology," to which Damrosch adds, "It would be ironic if literary scholars were to treat literature in ways that historians deplore as reductive" (11).

3. Most contemporary critics of the *Essay* are concerned to preserve, in some way, the value of the "ideas" in the poem. Douglas White, in *Pope and the Context of Controversy: The Manipulation of Ideas in "An Essay on Man"* (Chicago: University of Chicago Press, 1970), makes the interesting move of suggesting that Pope often expects his audience to know the arguments he is supporting or refuting. White concedes the presence of wit ("This element of wit has seldom if ever been emphasized in commentaries on the *Essay*") and mentions "the fluid, cajoling, and frequently almost chatty tone of the poem"; he adds that "the lugubriousness of the surface subject matter may hide the witty, bantering element of the poem from a twentieth-century audience" (9–10). However, he himself aims at casting light "on the conceptual vocabulary and intellectual sensitivities" of Pope's era (194), and he does not develop his perception of the presence of wit into any analytic form. Earlier, Thomas Edwards, Jr., in *This Dark Estate: A Reading of Pope* (Berkeley: University of California Press, 1963), argued (from the generic demands of the didactic poem) that "Pope was not a very gifted thinker; . . . by accepting the didactic role, he incurred an obligation to be rational that he could not fulfill . . . The poem is partly redeemed by just those aspects of temperament and sensibility that made Pope's didacticism unsuccessful" (28). He, too, makes no attempt at sustained analysis of Pope's wit in the *Essay*. A. D. Nuttall, in *Pope's "Essay on Man"* (London: George Allen & Unwin, 1984), attempts to redeem Pope as a didactic poet: the *Essay*, he says, "engages with a surprising number of major philosophical and theological cruces" (Preface; unnumbered page). Aside from fine descriptions of antithesis and zeugma, Nuttall does not analyze Pope's style at any length, and in fact becomes annoyed by it: "As the fifth section of the epistle [IV] comes to an end (lines 149 to 166) Pope's tone becomes almost testy . . . One wishes to pluck Pope by the sleeve and calm him . . . The second reason why the passage is ill-judged lies in the wholly inadvertent snub it gives to traditional Christianity" (158–159). The passage in question is one that parodies (in its pursuit of the

question why Vice should be allowed to prosper) the fencing give-and-take of Socratic dialogue as a speech-act. Although Reuben Brower's *Alexander Pope: The Poetry of Allusion* (Oxford: The Clarendon Press, 1959) says many good things in passing about Pope's "glissades," his irony, and his "athletic joy" in wit (215, 217, 231), the aim of the book is to compare Pope with his Roman precursors; and while describing the *Essay on Man* as "a free and original variation on the Horatian diatribe-epistle," Brower is on the whole unhappy with it, finding Pope more satisfactory in poems "where he felt less obliged to play the solemn philosopher" (239). He goes so far as to say that "Pope succeeded because he did not write the poem he seems to have thought he was writing" (212). This seems to me to underestimate Pope's own poetic intelligence. Although Patricia Meyer Spacks, in *An Argument of Images: The Poetry of Alexander Pope* (Cambridge, Mass.: Harvard University Press, 1971), argued for the substantiality and multiplicity of Pope's images, and G. S. Rousseau asserted in 1972 that there has been so much work on Pope's use of metaphor that "few critics will ever again read him as a poet of statement" ("On Reading Pope," in *Writers and Their Background: Alexander Pope,* ed. Peter Dixon [Ohio University Press, 1972], 19), subsequent books such as Nuttall's prove that the *Essay on Man* will always attract critics who want to understand it as a poem of statement. More recent studies of Pope have been less interested in style than in historical and cultural contexts, and are not germane to my purpose here.

4. *Letters of Alexander Pope,* Selected and with an Introduction by John Butt, from the text of George Sherburn (London: Oxford University Press, 1960), 5; subsequently cited as *Letters.*

5. My quotations are cited from the lightly modernized edition by William K. Wimsatt, *Alexander Pope: Selected Poetry and Prose* (New York: Holt, Rinehart and Winston, 1951, 1972).

6. It is immaterial (except for purposes of comparison) that Shaftesbury, one of Pope's sources, says almost this very thing in his *Characteristicks* (1732) [II, 304–305]: "'Why,' says one, 'was I not made by Nature strong as a Horse? Why not hardy and robust as the *Brute-Creature?*' . . . It were better . . . and more modest in him, to change the Expostulations and ask, 'Why was I not made in good earnest *a very* Brute?'" The excerpt from Shaftesbury reads as an earnest exemplum because the diction alternates between philosopher and interlocutor as the passage proceeds. In Pope, by contrast, the diction is invariant and reserved to the "homilist" in order to make the parodic verve of the poetic mirror-image apparent.

7. This line struck Emily Dickinson, who borrowed Pope's thunderbolt that stuns with music:

> What would the Dower be,
> Had I the Art to stun myself
> With Bolts – of Melody!

"I would not paint – a picture –": no. 348 in *The Poems of Emily Dickinson*, ed. R. W. Franklin (Cambridge, Mass.: The Belknap Press of Harvard University Press, 1998), 3 vols., I, 374.

8. This description of Pliny refers to his *Nat. Hist.* VII, 2.

9. Pliny, *The History of the World*, trans. Philemon Holland, Selected and Introduced by Paul Turner (London: Centaur Press, 1962), 77–78.

10. Maynard Mack, for instance, remarks in his Twickenham edition of the *Essay* (London: Methuen, 1950, lxxix–lxxx) that "Dryden's poem is genuinely ratiocinative, genuinely an argument, and everything about it accords with this: its tone is thoughtful, dispassionate, expository . . .; its arrangement is a series of different propositions leading up to conclusions." Although Mack remarks that "Pope's tone in the *Essay* is different," and that Pope's propositions occur "less as theorems than as formulations and definitions of states of mind," he nonetheless adheres to the notion of Pope as a poet of "the ideas most relevant to the theme of constructive renunciation—theodicy and ethics," and of "the rational passing over into mystery." He summarizes the "central meaning" of the *Essay* thus: "There is a fecundity and comprehensiveness in the Creation and in man himself which man cannot do justice to otherwise than by trusting it for what it is, and simultaneously an ideal order, unity, harmony, and purpose which man must both support and help to realize by disciplining himself." Mack gives to Pope's language, tones, paradoxes, and images only the function of "dramatiz[ing] the central meaning in the very texture of the verse." I would argue that the language, tones, and so forth juggle the ideas before us as spectacles rather than as articles for assent.

11. Yet each clause may also be said to differ from its companions. Each clause places capitalized abstractions as the subject of verbs, but the first two clauses set double nouns in subject position, while the latter two set a single noun in subject position. The other pleasing difference is the semantic variety in the verbs aligned in parallel: *answer, are, makes,* and *is.*

12. We notice that the four participles make a chiasmus, in which *doing* and *impelled* (the active verbals) bracket *suffering* and *checked* (the passive

ones); and though the active *doing* opens the first member of the summarizing couplet, the passive *slave* opens the second member. This arrangement contradicts that of the opening line of the passage, in which the first verb of the first member (horse) is a checking *(restrains)*, while the first verb of the second member (ox) is an impelling *(breaks)*.

13. According to Pope's friend Joseph Spence, Pope thought Montaigne's essay "Of the Inconsistency of our Actions" the best he wrote. Pope's remarks on Montaigne, as reported by Spence, read as follows: "Electricity seems to play upon all he writes; dramas of changeable states and passions flash before the mind; vivacities and volatilities dance before the attention, all in the interests of life's unpredictability." Spence observes, "Much as Pope insists on eternal order, and rests deeply assured of it, what takes his eye is the shotsilk of change, the 'light and darkness in our chaos join'd'" [*Essay on Man*, II, 203]. My quotations are taken from Joseph Spence's *Observations, Anecdotes, and Characters of Books and Men*, ed. James M. Osborn, 2 vols. (Oxford: Oxford University Press, 1966), 90.

14. See the intense reworking of the opening lines described (from the Morgan Library manuscript) by George Sherburn in "Pope at Work," in *Essays on the Eighteenth Century presented to David Nichol Smith* (Oxford: Oxford University Press, 1945), 49–64.

15. Pope himself commented on the best way to break the pentameter, pointing out that the most common breaks come after the fourth, fifth, or sixth syllable. He liked the fifth as the most unobtrusive. You could use several fifth-syllable breaks in a row, he said, and still seem natural; but repeated breaks at the fourth or sixth syllable risked becoming obvious. "Every Nice Ear must (I believe) have observ'd, that in any smooth English Verse of ten syllables, there is naturally a Pause either at the fourth, fifth, or sixth Syllable . . . Now I fancy, that to preserve an exact Harmony and Variety, none of these Pauses shou'd be continu'd above three lines together, without the Interposition of another; else it will be apt to weary the Ear with one continu'd Tone; at least it does mine" (To Henry Cromwell, November 25, 1710; *Letters*, 14).

16. *Letters* (To William Fortescue, June 7, 1733), 269.

17. As Pope wrote to Jonathan Swift after the completion of the *Essay on Man*, "I am almost at the end of my Morals, as I've been, long ago, of my Wit; my system is a short one, and my circle narrow. Imagination has no limits, and that is a sphere in which you may move on to eternity; but where one is confined to Truth (or to speak more like a human creature, to the ap-

pearances of Truth) we soon find the shortness of our Tether. Indeed by the help of a metaphysical chain of idaeas [*sic*], one may extend the circulation, go round and round for ever, without making any progress beyond the point to which Providence has pinn'd us: But this does not satisfy me, who would rather say a little to no purpose, than a great deal" (December 19, 1734; *Letters*, 278–279).

18. In the end, one returns with gratitude to Dr. Johnson's capitulation to Pope as a poet. Johnson criticized the *Essay* in some detail: "The *Essay on Man* was a work of great labour and long consideration, but certainly not the happiest of Pope's performances. The subject is perhaps not very proper for poetry, and the poet was not sufficiently master of his subject; metaphysical morality was to him a new study, he was proud of his acquisitions, and, supposing himself master of great secrets, was in haste to teach what he had not learned." But being Dr. Johnson he must, even against his own judgment, admit the "overwhelming pleasure" of reading Pope: "[The doctrines enunciated by Pope in the *Essay* were] never till now recommended by such a blaze of embellishment or such sweetness of melody. The vigorous contraction of some thoughts, the luxuriant amplification of others, the incidental illustrations, and sometimes the dignity, sometimes the softness of the verses, enchain philosophy, suspend criticism, and oppress judgement by overpowering pleasure." Samuel Johnson, *Lives of the English Poets*, ed. G. B. Hill, 3 vols. (Oxford: Clarendon Press, 1905), III, 242–243, 224.

2. Walt Whitman Thinking

1. From the sixth poem of the untitled twelve, later entitled "Faces." Quotations from Walt Whitman's *Leaves of Grass* in this chapter are taken from *Leaves of Grass*, Comprehensive Reader's Edition, ed. Harold W. Blodgett and Sculley Bradley (New York: New York University Press, 1965), henceforth referred to as *LG*. Dates of first publication are cited from this edition as well.

2. Published in Walt Whitman, *Notes and Fragments*, ed. R. M. Bucke (1899), I, 12; and cited in *LG*, 650.

3. Bucke, ed., *Notes and Fragments*, I, 28–29. Cited in *LG*, 705.

4. *The Correspondence of Henry Thoreau*, ed. W. Harding and G. Bode (New York: New York University Press, 1958), 444; George Santayana, *Interpretations of Poetry and Religion*, ed. W. Holzberger and Herman J. Saatkamp, Jr. (1900; reprinted, Cambridge, Mass.: MIT Press, 1989), 109.

5. Others include, by a rough survey, and by somewhat elastic criteria: "Youth, Day, Old Age and Night" (1855); "To You" (1860); "Not Heat Flames Up and Consumes" (1860); "Sometimes with One I Love" (1860); "Among the Multitude" (1860); "What Am I After All" (1860); "Who Is Now Reading This?" (1860); "You Felons on Trial in Courts" (original version, 1860; subsequent editions deleted the first three stanzas); "Says," section 7 (1860); "Full of Life Now" (1860); "Pensive on Her Dead Gazing" (1865); "Camps of Green" (1865); "Look Down Fair Moon" (1865); "Adieu to a Soldier" (1871); "By Broad Potomac's Shore" (1872); "Souvenirs of Democracy" (1872); "My Legacy" (1872); "Wandering at Morn" (1873); "To a Locomotive in Winter" (1876); "Twilight" (1887); "A Font of Type" (1888); "After the Dazzle of Day" (1888); and "Grand is the Seen" (1891).

6. An explicit expression by Whitman of this detached "musing" state of mind is given in the uncollected poem "Mask with Their Lids" and in the prose note preceding it (c. 1870), printed in Walt Whitman, *LG*, 672, 672n.:

> Mask with their lids thine eyes, O Soul!
> The standards of the light & sense shut off
> To darkness now retiring, inward from abysms,
> The objective world behind thee left,
> How curious, looking thence, appears the world, appear thy
>   comrades,
> Appears aloof thy life, each passion, each event.
> And this thy visage [of thyself]?

The prose note runs as follows: "Let the piece 'Droop-droop thine eyes, O Soul'—convey the idea of a trance, yet with all the senses alert—only a state of high exalted musing—the tangible & material with all its shows—the objective world suspended or surmounted for a while & the powers in exaltation, freedom, vision—yet the *senses* not lost or contemn'd—Then chant, celebrate the unknown, the future hidden spiritual world—the real reality."

7. See the passage (subsequently dropped) following line 17 of canto 10, in the first (1856) printing of "By Blue Ontario's Shore," in which Whitman says of the "American literat":

> As he emits himself, facts are showered over with light,
>   The day-light is lit with more volatile light—the deep between the
>   setting and rising sun goes deeper many fold,

> Each precise object, condition, combination, process, exhibits a
>   beauty—the multiplication-table its, old age its, the carpenter's
>   trade its. [*LG,* 629]

8. See, for example, the note on the poem (390n.) by the editors of the
Comprehensive Reader's Edition of *Leaves of Grass:* "The poet . . . bring[s] in
himself as observer, conscious perhaps of himself as being also a maker of
sparkles from the wheel."

9. Whitman could not write such a counter-poem, because it is difficult
for him to create the figure of a father who loves his son. His own father (as
we see him anonymously in "There Was a Child Went Forth") was "mean,
anger'd, unjust."

10. Lest it be thought anomalous to interpret Whitman's secular poem in
terms of Faith, Hope, and (subsequently) Love—the Christian theological
virtues—I cite Whitman's plan for a poem in a pre-1855 notebook (Library
of Congress, *Walt Whitman: Catalog Based upon the Collections,* 85), in which,
for Love, Whitman substitutes—since it is to be the poem of an old man—
Joy: "Poem incarnating the mind of an old man . . . the utterance of hope
and floods of anticipation—faith in whatever happens—but all enfolded; Joy
Joy Joy which underlies and overtops the whole effusion." Cited in *LG,* 177n.

11. One can imagine (with apologies to Whitman) such a ballad, con-
structed from the "same" materials:

> Come up from the fields, Father,
> Here's a letter just now come,
> And come to the door, mother,
> Here's a letter from your son.
>
> The father comes at the call,
> The mother speeds to the door,
> She opens the letter quickly,
> Will she see her son once more?
>
> The daughter says, "Grieve not, Mother,
> Our Pete will soon be better";
> The little sisters are weeping,
> They tremble at the letter.
>
> The broken sentences follow:
> *Gunshot wound in the breast,*

> *Cavalry skirmish, hospital—*
> *Will soon be better with rest.*
>
> He will never be better, poor lad,
> The boy is already dead.
> The mother sinks to the floor,
> Her heart is fainting in dread.
>
> Presently, dressed in black,
> She will mourn till life is done,
> Waking, weeping, wishing,
> To follow her dear dead son.

In a ballad version, no narratorial "effusing" can take place; narrative objectivity rules.

12. Philip Fisher, in *Still the New World* (Cambridge, Mass.: Harvard University Press, 1999, chapter 2, passim), discusses what he regards as Whitman's "appropriation" of the voices of other Americans, his "impersonation" of them, saying, with respect to the famous line "I was the man, I suffer'd, I was there" and other such verses: "Whitman turns [his countrymen] into an audience of idle observers of his enthusiastic substitution of himself for them" (83). This is—though Fisher does not say so—the very characteristic of lyric: to incorporate all of reality into a single speaking voice. The familiar complaint that "people" are absent from a given poet's lyrics (an accusation made, for instance, by Mark Halliday regarding the work of Wallace Stevens) misunderstands the nature of lyric, as does the assertion of "appropriation" of the voices of others. Lyric must express social content through a *single* voice encompassing response universally.

13. "In the Feinberg Collection [of the Library of Congress] are two MS pages containing a list of about ninety words expressive of sorrow, evidently compiled by the poet in working on ["When Lilacs Last in the Dooryard Bloom'd"]." *LG,* 328n.

14. Quoted in Herbert Bergman, "Ezra Pound and Walt Whitman," *American Literature, 27* (March 1955), 60.

3. Emily Dickinson Thinking

1. Emily Dickinson, "The Outer – from the Inner" [450; 1862]. I cite Dickinson's poems by first line and number and date from *The Poems of Em-*

ily Dickinson, Variorum Edition, ed. R. W. Franklin (Cambridge, Mass.: The Belknap Press of Harvard University Press, 1998), 3 vols. However, I silently substitute *its* for Dickinson's characteristic misspelling *it's,* and *upon* for Dickinson's *opon,* both retained by Franklin. I do not find any compelling reason, given my purposes here, to use the designations "fascicles" and "sets" to refer to the groupings of Dickinson's poems.

2. All of Dickinson's critics have had something to say about her structuring of time. The most insightful account in this respect remains that of Sharon Cameron in *Lyric Time: Dickinson and the Limits of Genre* (Baltimore: Johns Hopkins University Press, 1979). Although Cameron calls attention to some of the restructurings of time in Dickinson, she does so to further a theoretical claim: that lyric can really tolerate only a single tense, the present. Her aim is to conflate poems to this model; my aim is to distinguish them from each other in their revision of temporal structures.

3. The word "aftermath," used by David Porter in *Dickinson: The Modern Idiom* (Cambridge, Mass.: Harvard University Press, 1981), 12, and initially proposed in his 1974 article "The Crucial Experience in Emily Dickinson's Poetry" (*ESQ: A Journal of the American Renaissance,* 77 [1974], 280–290), has been widely adopted in Dickinson criticism because it covers both the poems which adopt a posthumous voice and others, such as "After great pain," which do not.

4. Here the verbs are, successively, *lap, lick, stop, feed, step, peer, pare, crawl, chase,* and *neigh,* before coming to an end at *stop.*

5. The whole poem "Bound – a trouble –" is significant for my argument, since in it Dickinson states her conviction that life is bearable only if one is told that suffering (measured out, as her dashes show, drop by bleeding drop, in a chromatism heading toward exsanguination) eventually will come to an end. She imagines counting off the time till its end (the setting sun) by "notching" it moment by moment, as on a primitive calendar-stick:

> Bound – a trouble –
> And lives can bear it!
> Limit – how deep a bleeding go!
> So – many – drops – of vital scarlet –
> Deal with the soul
> As with Algebra!
>
> Tell it the Ages – to a cypher –
> And it will ache – contented – on –

> Sing – at its pain – as any Workman –
> Notching the fall of the even sun! [240 A; 1861]

To "deal with the soul / As with Algebra" is, for Dickinson, to arrange it in a continuous line such as that found on a graph in which time is plotted against some other variable, such as drops of blood.

6. Other inch-by-inch chromaticisms strive for pure motion not only by omitting the *and then*'s but also by including a multiple number of implied sequences, as in "The Love a Child can show – below –" in which the poet remarks of temporality:

> 'Tis this – invites – appalls – endows –
> Flits – glimmers – proves – dissolves –
> Returns – suggests – convicts – enchants –
> Then – flings in Paradise! [285; 1862–63]

Rearranged in their four individual serial groups, these verbs will read:

(1) invites – appalls
(2) endows – flits
(3) glimmers – proves – dissolves
(4) returns – suggests – convicts – enchants – then – flings in Paradise

The first three of these "disappointing" sequences are "regular" in their temporally logical inceptions and closures, whether expressed in binary (Beginning and End) or ternary (Beginning, Middle, and End) form. The final sequence, however, is one in which, after ending, the past is resurrected (when that which has dissolved "returns"). A second happy ending follows, in which the final "clearing in the road" is Paradise. As in this case, Dickinson will often reduce plot—while maintaining its chromaticism—to two or three essential "steps": "Born – Bridalled – Shrouded – / In a Day –" ["Title divine – is mine!" 194; 1861]. The point is still exhaustiveness—the idea is to omit no *indispensable* step in the process, even if one has reduced the number of steps to the crucial ones alone.

7. Are there, then, no chromatic poems of seriality after 1863? Yes, there are; but they have mostly become epistemologically innocuous, by the suppression of analogy to human experience, which must end in death or bafflement. Because sequence has no inner consequence for harmless natural phenomena, such as the rain, active verbs can return in a delighted set of

"ribbons," as in, for example, the 1872 poem "Like Rain it sounded till it curved":

> That was indeed the Rain –
> It filled the Wells, it pleased the Pools
> It warbled in the Road –
> It pulled the spigot from the Hills
> And let the Floods abroad – [1245; 1872]

Dickinson shrinks from imagining a tragic result, such as the destruction of human beings, occurring because of the rainfall, and presses thought to leap to another plane rather than follow the sequence it has initiated out to deluge. Thus, when she makes the rain cease, Dickinson resorts to the analogy of Elijah's translation from the earthly plane to a heavenly one:

> It loosened acres, lifted seas
> The sites of Centres stirred
> Then like Elijah rode away
> Upon a Wheel of Cloud.

And in the poem that immediately follows in Franklin's edition, while on the earthly plane thunder and lightning destroy forests (but not habitations or human beings), the dead, in their subterranean graves, are, like Elijah, immune to the disasters of sequence:

> The Thunder crumbled like a stuff
> How good to be in Tombs
> Where nature's Temper cannot reach
> Nor missile ever comes. [1246; 1872]

8. Sharon Cameron reads "out of Sound" as meaning "out of hearing." This is perhaps tenable, but it does not account for the irruption of actual sound into a hitherto soundless poem. Nor do balls of yarn go "out of Sound" when they fall to the floor. I believe Dickinson is thinking of the sequence of sound in music when she generates this line. A manuscript variant offers a more logical remark to make of falling balls of yarn: they go not "out of Sound" but "out of Reach." Another revealing variant exists for lines 5–6:

> The Dust behind, I strove to join
> Unto the Disk before.

The metaphors make clear the spherical beauty of the earlier "formed" Disk—thought—and the organic incoherence of the next would-be Disk—thought which has turned to Dust, disintegrating in atoms that cannot be "joined" to the circlet of former thoughts.

9. To "finish knowing" seems to me unambiguous; once one is reduced to numbness of mind, silence, and only one organ ("Being, but an Ear"), there is nowhere to go but to the obliteration of consciousness. Some commentators have wanted to believe that the speaker may, now that she has finished "knowing," have other possibilities for cognitive self-esteem. I cannot see any room for such possibilities after the "funeral," and the failure of "Reason."

10. This line puzzles Cameron (*Lyric Time*, 168), who finds it "redundant": "The stanza's final line boldly flaunts its own redundancy. 'A Quartz contentment' is 'like a stone –' because quartz is a stone." Rather, quartz is a vitreous crystal, as Dickinson would have known from her scientific reading if not from her lexicon.

11. Cameron, unlike other commentators, reads the final simile as a return to feeling: "The 'letting go –' is not a letting go of life, is not death, but is rather the more colloquial 'letting go' of feeling, an unleashing of the ability to experience it again" (*Lyric Time*, 169). I find this improbable: the freezing persons are on their way to being frozen. The fact that they are part of a simile of survival does not mean that their *recollection* is one of survival. Rather, they recollect the last phase before unconsciousness, before their consciousness lapsed altogether.

12. If Dickinson cannot preserve serial temporality after death, she hopes to preserve motion at least, and this leads to her imagining a burial in the "tumultuous" sea (the "swinging sea" in one manuscript variant), in which the stiff sitting of "After great pain" could not possibly occur:

> Fortitude incarnate
> Here is laid away
> In the swift Partitions
> Of the awful Sea –
>
> . . .
>
> Edifice of Ocean
> Thy tumultuous Rooms

Suit me at a venture
Better than the Tombs [1255; 1872]

13. See Jack Lee Capps, *Emily Dickinson's Reading, 1836–1886* (Cambridge, Mass.: Harvard University Press, 1966).

14.   Crumbling is not an instant's Act
A fundamental pause
Dilapidation's processes
Are Organized Decays –

    'Tis first a Cobweb on the Soul
A Cuticle of Dust
A Borer in the Axis
An Elemental Rust –

    Ruin is formal – Devil's work
Consecutive and slow –
Fail in an instant, no man did
Slipping – is Crashe's law.

15. See Dickinson's comment on the "algebra" of emotion in "Bound – a trouble –" quoted in note 5.

16. Dickinson's serio-comic recipe for self-revision can be found in "These are the nights that beetles love":

    A Bomb upon the Ceiling
Is an improving thing –
It keeps the nerves progressive
Conjecture flourishing – [1150; 1868]

17. It even seems to Dickinson, occasionally, that the dead are the truly alive ones, and we the dead:

    As we – it were – that perished –
Themself – had just remained till we rejoin them –
And 'twas they, and not ourself
That mourned – [337; 1862]

18. Written to her aunt Catherine, whose son Henry died on February 17, 1870.

19. One can imagine (with apologies to the poem) a lyric that would track, in Dickinson's earlier, chronological, chromatic, step-by-step order,

the successive lengthening of the shadows and the failing of the shaft of light:

> When we see a Shaft of Light
> Slanting through the Trees –
> On a Winter afternoon
> Weighing on our Eyes –
>
> Then we feel, within our Brain –
> A Cathedral Tune –
> As the steady Shadows – lean –
> Darker – into Dim –
>
> Then Light fading – fainter still –
> Tells us of Despair –
> As the Landscape vanishes
> In the somber Air –
>
> Till the ones who held their Breath,
> Watching ebbing Light –
> Still afflicted – perish – with it –
> At the fall of Night –

The predictability of such a fading prevents our feeling (as we do when reading Dickinson's actual poem) the sudden wounding oppression of the heart by the oblique light, and the consequent necessity of Dickinson's subsequent analytic move.

20. See the Pauline poem "The things we thought that we should do," with the stasis of its monotone serial rhyme in -un, which denies the possibility of change:

> The things we thought that we should do
> We other things have done
> But those peculiar industries
> Have never been begun.
>
> The Lands we thought that we should seek
> When large enough to run
> By Speculation ceded
> To Speculation's Son –

The Heaven, in which we hoped to pause
When Discipline was done
Untenable to Logic
But possibly the one – [1279; 1873–76, Version D]

Dickinson's manuscript alternatives in line 11 to the intellectual *untenable* are the more material and metaphorical *impassable* and *impervious*. The ingenuity by which each stanza undoes by inaction its earlier thinking ("we thought . . . we thought . . . we hoped") of the life-narrative it wishes it could have told (*doing, seeking, pausing*) is a final parody of the serial chromatic order. This is a serial order in which nothing envisioned is accomplished, an order of preemptive *un*-doing (hence the punning choice of "*un*-tenable").

4. W. B. Yeats Thinking

1. I cite this poem and subsequent ones in this chapter from *The Variorum Edition of the Poems of W. B. Yeats,* ed. Peter Allt and Russell Alspach (New York: Macmillan, 1987).

2. See "The Scholars" on "lines / Rhymed out in love's despair / To flatter Beauty's ignorant ear."

3. Cited from Thomas Parkinson, *W. B. Yeats: The Later Poetry* (Berkeley: University of California Press, 1964), who discusses the manuscripts of "Among School Children" on pp. 92–113. This citation is from p. 107. *The Tower* has not yet appeared in the Cornell Edition of Yeats's manuscripts.

4. The applicable lines (1–8) of Sonnet 24 are:

Mine eye hath played the painter and hath stelled
Thy beauty's form in table of my heart;
My body is the frame wherein 'tis held,
And pérspective it is best painter's art.
For through the painter must you see his skill
To find where your true image pictured lies,
Which in my bosom's shop is hanging still,
That hath his windows glazèd with thine eyes.

Index

Keats, John, 2
Konner, Melvin, 122n2

Leda, 96, 101
Locke, John, 18
Logan, William, 121n2

Mack, Maynard, 11, 125n10
Milton, John, 82, 107
Montaigne, Michel de, 17, 27; "Of the Inconsistency of our Actions," 126n13

New Criticism, 3
New Historicism, 5
Nicodemus, 77–78
Nuttall, A. D., 123n3

Oisin, 110, 112–114, 116

Parkinson, Thomas, 136n3
Pascal, Blaise, 29
Paul, St., 60, 136n20
Plato, 12, 15, 84, 96–97, 101–102, 107
Pliny, 16
Pope, Alexander, 7–9, 10–36, 118–119; dismissal of, 10–12, 35–36; use of parody/satire, 13–16, 18, 20–21, 35; physiological speculation, 15–16; ideas in poetry, 16–18, 20–21, 26–27; depiction of Golden Age, 18–20; syntactic procedures, 22–27, 32–33, 36; living thought, 27; image of man, 28–35; rhythms of thinking, 31–34, 36; representation of thought, 34–35
WORKS: *Epistle to Dr. Arbuthnot,* 10; *Essay on Man,* 7, 10–36, 122n1, 123n3, 125n10, 127n18

Porphyry, 107
Porter, David, 131n3
Pound, Ezra, 63
Putnam, Hilary, 122n2
Pythagoras, 97, 101

Ransom, John Crowe, 3
Renaissance, 99, 115
Richards, I. A., 3–4
Romanticism, 115
Rousseau, George, 122n2, 124n3

Santayana, George, 8, 38, 41
Schorske, Carl, 123n2
Shaftesbury, Earl of (Anthony Ashley Cooper), 18, 29, 124n6
Shakespeare, William: *Antony and Cleopatra,* 104; *Hamlet,* 28; *King Lear,* 79; sonnet 24, 115, 137n4
Sherburn, George, 126n14
Shklar, Judith, 122n2
Socrates, 12
Spacks, Patricia Meyer, 124n3
Spence, John, 126n13
Spenser, Edmund, 18
Stevens, Wallace, 8–9, 30, 122n4, 130n12; "Sunday Morning," 8
Swift, Jonathan, 127n18

Tasso, Torquato, 99
Tate, Allen, 3
Thoreau, Henry David, 38

Vaughan, Henry, 78
Vitruvius, 31

Wakefield, Gilbert: *Observations on Pope,* 16
Warburton, William, 29
Warren, Robert Penn, 3
White, Douglas, 123n3